PSYCHOSIS IN THE FAMILY

Other titles in the UKCP Series:

PSYCHOSIS IN THE FAMILY

The Journey of a Transpersonal Psychotherapist and Mother

Janet C. Love

On behalf of the United Kingdom Council
for Psychotherapy

KARNAC

First published in 2009 by
Karnac Books Ltd
118 Finchley Road, London NW3 5HT

British Library Cataloguing in Publication Data

A C.I.P. for this book is available from the British Library

ISBN-13: 978 1 85575 520 8

Edited, designed and produced by The Studio Publishing Services Ltd,
www.publishingservicesuk.co.uk
e-mail: studio@publishingservicesuk.co.uk

Printed in Great Britain

www.karnacbooks.com

CONTENTS

ACKNOWLEDGEMENTS

To my son
and to the unsung heroine of the book,
my daughter

And to all my fellow journeymen who made this book possible by sharing their stories.

However, I would never had the courage to put pen to paper without Joyce Ferguson, who has supported me unfailingly and offered her professional guidance on the importance of personal narrative for cultural change. To Clea Sambrook, I give my heartfelt thanks for her invaluable support and assistance for being the mid-wife of this work. Last but not least, I thank Annie Gargya for her teacher's red pen denoting the colour of the heart.

ABOUT THE AUTHOR

Janet C. Love began her career as a self employed interior designer. She changed career midlife to become an internal designer of another kind, and retrained as a transpersonal psychotherapist.

She founded and supports a charity called "Loving Someone in Psychosis". Their aim is to promote the voice of the family and friends to help their loved ones.

She now works in private practice as a family constellation therapist, transpersonal psychotherapist (UKCP and MBACP), and autogenic therapist (dip. AT). More information can be found at www.loveconstellationtherapy.com, or by e-mailing Janet at janetclove@janetclove.com

PREFACE

Psychosis is a psychiatric collective term for severe psychological diseases. Someone who experiences psychosis has little chance of release or relief. There is a danger of life-long dependence on medication and of living a life not integrated in society. This is an unbearable condition for all those affected, as well for their relatives. Society as a whole must not be allowed to close its eyes in the face of such suffering and hopelessness.

My psychotherapeutic work with psychotic clients, particularly through the use of the constellation method, has helped me to develop and gain a deeper understanding of the origins of patterns of psychosis, and the awful experiences, thoughts, and crazy behaviours that emanate from this.

At the root of the development of psychosis lies an emotionally unbearable experience, a particular form of trauma. This traumatic event is held hidden in the family system, but is transmitted unconsciously over generations in the care-giving relationships and through emotional bonding.

Psychosis can be a great catastrophe in a family. It brings all its members to the edge of craziness. It also offers a chance for all involved to acknowledge the traumas of the past and grow out of and beyond them, in order to heal psychologically and solve the traumatic past of the family in the best sense possible.

Janet Love, the mother of a son who had psychosis, went this way to face the suppressed painful experiences within her family. This is an exceptional achievement. Her example can give courage and hope to others to walk this path, too. From my varied therapeutical experiences with families, the sorrow of the family is often manifested in the psychosis in one family member. I know that psychoses are actually curable through the constellation process.

Franz Ruppert
Professor of Psychology at the University of Applied Sciences, Munich
March 2009

NOTE TO THE READER

The twenty-first century has seen a significant shift among us to take more personal responsibility for our illnesses. The Internet has largely contributed to this by offering us unlimited information on the diagnosis and treatments of all medical conditions. To date, severe mental illness has been a particularly closed book, with only psychiatrists and mental health professionals knowing its secrets and mysteries. In particular, psychosis and schizophrenia, involving extreme and altered states of consciousness have been subjects which for centuries have lain behind the locked doors of the experts, just as the severely mentally ill have been hidden away in institutions in a continuing denial that they belong to the human family. The dominant expert discourses on psychiatry have thus silenced the voices of those most closely affected by psychosis: the family. My narrative, as both a mother and a transpersonal psychotherapist, is another kind of "expert" story, drawing on both my personal and professional direct experiences. My story is not intended to replace professional expert knowledge, but to place alongside it another voice to form a larger narrative than has previously been available.

Psychosis in the Family. The loving family was mine, and the psychosis belonged to my son. The timing of his illness coincided with the third year of my five-year training to be a transpersonal psychotherapist. The transpersonal approach seeks to acknowledge, yet move beyond, the awareness of the individual "self" as a separate, isolated consciousness. It seeks to embrace a more interrelated, universal, and complex sense of being which is in harmony with an unseen order of things. It recognizes that there exists beyond ourselves a powerful force that nurtures our growth and evolution.

When my son's illness came knocking at my door, I found myself without a map or a signpost for the psycho-spiritual journey ahead. Loving someone in psychosis means that when we most want to reach out to our loved ones, we are stripped of our previous tools of communication, namely, logic and the language of a presumed shared experience of objective reality. Stripped and isolated, we then often suffer the second blow of the illness: the stigma. This is the isolating and devastating journey we find ourselves on, which is ultimately and intimately bound to the journey of our loved ones.

Through my psychotherapy training, I found myself personally challenged to see if I could find some kind of meaning in these desperate times. At the same time, I had also become aware, through Freud's unique contribution to psychotherapy, that we are all, in fact, the products of unconscious and uncontrollable forces in the mind. Therefore, I found myself beginning to evaluate my own unconscious responses rather than judge my son's.

Finally, seeking to create what I most wanted to find, I ran a weekend workshop, "Does Someone You Love Have Schizophrenia?" Here, in a safe and supportive environment, kindred spirits could share their experiences without fear of stigma or shame. The shared benefits within the group inspired me and reinforced my belief that we did not have a voice. This book is my testament to that experience and the focus of my therapeutic work changed in this direction.

My main priority, however, was to help my son avoid a life-long sentence of drug-controlled mental illness. I could not believe, in these alternative times, that there seemed to be very little on offer outside conventional psychiatric care. Against all the odds, I pursued and researched holistic approaches to his illness.

In the same period, my widowed mother was diagnosed with dementia. Her previous history was of a lifetime of depression and obsessive–compulsive disorder. As an only child, it was another mantle I had to take on. Just as I had fought so hard for a holistic approach for my son, I found myself in the polar opposite position of begging for psychiatric help for my mother. I wanted any mind-altering drugs which would help and offer respite from the difficult and non-negotiable personality traits I found myself subjected to. To hell with understanding my unconscious responses, these were difficult times that I could not manage. A more discerning and richer understanding of the impact of mental illness on the family became apparent. I began to realize how much my learnt personality had been shaped by my mother's mental illness.

However, before I begin my story, I believe it is important to be clear about the nature of the telling. It is an autoethnographic text (auto, i.e., self; ethos, i.e., culture; graphy, i.e., the research process), a provocative weave of story and theory, using reflexive research. This means that my own experiences and their context inform the inquiry. It is meant to reveal not just what I discovered, but how I discovered it. It offers some information and resources for nutritional and holistic approaches to psychosis to support and enhance orthodox psychiatry. It is a personal and therapeutic evaluation of both conscious and unconscious responses to altered states of reality. It also deals with the eternally thorny question of family involvement in, or detachment from, the treatment of psychosis. However it is even more than that; it is an inquiry into how unconscious forces influence our minds, our bodies, and the entire family system. Its premise is that if we cannot understand our own responses, how can we understand those of our loved ones? The inquiry is done with humility, and an understanding that the contents revealed do not speak alone. It leaves much unsaid and is woefully incomplete given the vastness of the subject. It is, at best, the book I most wanted to find on the bookshelves in my darkest hour; a book written not just by a professional, but by someone who had walked the heart-rending path of experiencing the psychological trauma of loving someone in an altered state.

Therefore, by defining the book as my personal quest to understand how to help my son, it becomes clear that it is not a story about him. That is his story, for him to tell at the right time, space, and sequence. I have no desire to expose him in any way, for I have only respect, admiration, and downright awe at the way he has handled this aspect of his life. So if, in the reading, you feel that some of the details of his symptoms are not explicit, that is my direct intention. By the same token, the fall-out effects on the rest of the immediate family, my daughter and ex-husband, are not included. Their responses remain just that. I bow before their own pain, and their ways of dealing with it. My wholly different response to my mother's dementia, on top of her existing mental illnesses, underpin, interweave with, and enrich the main story. Finally, I also include, with their permission, some of my clients' experiences to gain a broader perspective than just my own.

In conclusion, I offer my unique story to you with the understanding that, of course, it will differ in content from any other. It is a story of loving someone and often failing them. However, in the telling of my story, I would like to challenge the idea that psychosis in the family is a subject too terrible and shameful to be told. It is my hypothesis that psychosis also happens to warm, sane, loving people and their families.

Janet C. Love

CHAPTER ONE

Drawing the line

Diary extract

Schizophrenia is the cruellest disease of the Western world. It afflicts young adults, often beginning insidiously and progressing until the ambitions, potentials, and hopes of early years are disregarded in disarray. In their place lie broken thoughts, inappropriate or stunted emotions, and internal voices or other misperceptions that can make existence a living hell (Torrey, 1980, p. 3).

Some days are etched indelibly on the soul. So it was on that pale grey Tuesday in August, a day so unremarkable for its weather that wearing summer clothes was a mere token of illusion. Our small flat in Islington had a large terrace with table and chairs, and pots and plants, but there seemed nothing to entice us outside except the lack of space inside.

It is one of the great delusions of life itself that, as we get up each day, we think we can plan what is going to happen. I had no idea that I would be forever changed by the experiences of that day. The fact that I had missed and denied all the tell-tale signs that led up to it still does not reduce its significance. (Even as I write these words now, I pause at the keyboard and instinctively find myself with my hand over my mouth. Can I really write this stuff to share with you?)

And so it came to pass, the uttering of those first words by my son: nothing more sinister than that. No weird actions, no strange behaviour, just that one sentence that confirmed my worst fears. That singular moment when I knew for absolute certain that he had crossed the line from living in consensus reality into an altered state.

In the real world, I was rendered speechless. This was my intelligent, articulate, eloquent son. I did not challenge it or confront it, but I felt a leaden, sinking sensation in my heart and an ominous silence hung in the air. It was a sentence that would be followed by many other sentences. But it was the sentence of condemnation that I heard so clearly, the deafening clash of the prison gates. The sentence of living with altered states of reality was upon us.

I pause again at the keyboard as I relive these events. I want to rerun the video, somehow make it different. Not this, not my son. But I knew, deep inside me I knew. It was the inevitability of our sentence of suffering that felt so overwhelming. It left me feeling there was nowhere to run, nowhere to hide. The *terra firma* of my life simply dropped away from beneath me. I entered the realm of those who have to suffer doubly, having to watch the loved one suffer and not being allowed to have any problems of their own. There I was, right on track for my own individual customized version of "living hell". Psychosis had driven its mighty sword into my former familiar, cosy, dysfunctional existence.

Minutes later I left the flat and ran out into a nearby park, mercifully empty of people. Those etched moments come back to me so clearly. Everything was stark and in frightening detail, each veined leaf and broken twig that lay on that cracked tarmac path seeming as if they had lain in wait for me for all eternity, waiting for just that very moment. Dazed and confused I rang my ex-husband to try to describe the enormity of what had just happened and what I thought it meant. His was a perfectly natural reaction at this stage. Was it, in fact, me who was mad? Had I heard correctly? How could I be sure? My head swirled, and so began the turmoil of my new existence: what was real and what was imagined? My thoughts became incoherent; I could make no sense of the events of the morning, the telephone call, the empty park.

And then it was time to make lunch; anything, anything to try to take a step backwards into ordinary, everyday normality. And a normal lunch it was, except for my feeling that the entire contents of my stomach had been emptied out on to the floor. Perhaps it was only one sentence. Everything seemed fine. It might go away.

And soon it was the afternoon, and I had to go to see two therapy clients. I could not cancel them at this late stage. I was, in some ways, relieved to have something concrete to do. I drove from North to West London in a kind of fog. After parking the car, I rang the World Healing Crusade in Blackpool. This is an organization that prays continually for those in need. My mother-in-law had always used them in times of crisis for our family. She believed every family crisis had been averted through their prayers. I placed my son's name on the Sanctuary. My God, I needed all the help I could get. My own ability to pray was very far removed from conscious awareness at this time.

I was going to my psychotherapy training college in Little Venice. A large cream building overlooking the canal basin, the home of soul-directed therapy, peopled by caring, conscious therapists, a refuge for the troubled in spirit. I fell through its familiar large, tall doors. Normally busy and alive, on this grey day in August, its corridors were empty and eerily quiet. I went straight to reception to ask the secretary which therapists were in that afternoon. I told her I was having a crisis and my own therapist was on a six-week summer break. I leant on the reception desk and felt it temporarily holding me up. I was desperate. I needed to talk. Why do crises always happen at holiday times?

I came out from working with my own clients. The secretary told me one of the psychotherapists could see me now. Mercifully, it was my very own supervisor, a highly experienced and wise therapist and a director of the college. We went into room ten, our familiar supervisory space, but today the air was different. Its normal healing atmosphere and my supervisor's steady presence did not calm my jangled self. But hang on a minute: I knew from his lectures that one of his sons had schizophrenia and had been in and out of institutions all his life. The thoughts raced in my mind. Was this a cosmic joke? I had the right person to talk to, he knew this story, he had walked this journey. But he was the wrong person too. I did not want this for my son. But I did not tell him this. The chaotic thoughts stayed within me. He listened well, as ever. He asked me to notice if my son was sleeping all right. He said, "Anyone can make one delusional remark." He counselled me to be watchful. He gave me the name of a therapist for my son, who trained with R. D. Laing. As I left the room, he hugged me. Our professional relationship of three years had gone out of the window. In that hug, I knew I was in for a stormy ride. His normal wise words, "You are living in interesting times," did not make it into the session once.

Back in the street, I went for my car. It was not there. I could not think straight. I spotted a traffic warden and dimly realized that I had only paid for two hours. He came over to me, wafting my fine and details of the car pound. A more compassionless person I had yet to encounter. All my anger of the day was silently vented towards him. I took a taxi to the car pound. There, lined up among hundreds of cars, was mine. I vaguely wondered what had happened to all those other people on this momentous day. I went to the desk with my official documents and looked into the cold, uncaring eyes of the fines collector person. I paid my massive cheque for the unspeakable sin of forgetting the time while the world tumbled around my ears. So soon after ringing the World Healing Crusade, I wondered if there was a God at all.

I drove home and into the underground car park of my block of flats, with its tight parking spaces and concrete columns. As I reversed into my designated parking slot, I completely misjudged the space, and scraped the driver's side of the car. The sound of the cold hard metal scraping against the hard cold concrete seemed to echo the portent of doom I felt in my soul. Another hundred pounds at least. But I did not care. I did not even stop to investigate. All I cared about was getting back to see my son, to make sure he was all right.

Back into the flat, all my sensory antennae on red alert. All seemed well, quiet even. But already I had been active in looking for ways to help us. My previous interest in holistic medicine now came to the fore. My daughter had been out, on my instructions, to find a complementary medicine book on mental illness. Up to that point, I had absolutely no idea of what might be available. She had bought *Nutrition and Mental Illness: An Orthomolecular Approach to Balancing Body Chemistry* (1987), by Carl C. Pfeiffer, PhD, MD. On that dark day, it was such a relief to read the wording on the back of the book, offering some hope that my ingrained belief that schizophrenia was an incurable disease of unknown causes might not be the case.

> A pioneer in the field of nutritional research, Dr Carl Pfeiffer has found nutritional therapies successful in abating and even over-coming many psychological disorders, from anxiety and depression to phobias and schizophrenia. In his extensive research into the connection between nutrition and mental illness, Dr Pfeiffer has clearly shown that a proper biochemical balance within the body is the key to maintaining good mental as well as physical health. Believing that anti-psychotic drugs actually pose obstacles to the long-term healing process, Dr. Pfeiffer corrects the chemical imbalances that contribute to psychiatric disturbances by adjusting the diets of his patients and prescribing large doses of essential vitamins, minerals and trace elements.

The die was cast. That first book, those initial words indicating that anti-psychotic drugs actually posed problems to the long-term healing process, fed into my own constructs of belief. Despite my lack of knowledge of nutritional research, my fear of psychiatric institutions, albeit without a base in reality, took me over. An integrated route was what I wanted to pursue.

Another evening, another so-called normal meal, nothing strange to report. But a new me was there, the new hyper-vigilant me, watching and waiting. That evening in bed, my mind could make no sense of the day. My body, however, had acquired a new, subtle kind of weight. I wondered as I lay looking at that damn magnolia ceiling, if I would ever laugh again.

A new day, and with it came the announcement from my son that he had not slept all night.

Reflections on drawing the line

And that line that you see across the page is simply how it was. A line had been drawn across my life, before that day and after that day, a line that marked the thin veil between consensus reality and altered states of reality. The line where I felt brutally catapulted from the world that values only the sane and bright and healthy into the shadows and hinterlands of the unconscious reality of psychosis. I would be forever changed by that line. How would it change me, where would it lead me? Would it ultimately strengthen me or weaken me?

Of course, those twenty-four hours did not present themselves without many signs, symptoms, and warning signals in the preceding months. This was not the beginning of the illness, but it was my recognition of it. However, it was not the recognition that prompted me to share those twenty-four hours with you, but the psychological trauma that the arrival of the symptoms heralded deep within me. The broken thoughts described by Torrey at the beginning of the chapter were now my very own. I felt as if the world I knew had disintegrated. Paradoxically, I also had one moment of undistorted immediate experience in that day. When my son spoke that first sentence that did not concur with external reality, a deep loyalty to him and his illness just welled up in me. They were not his words. They were just the first recognizable symptoms of the illness. There rose in me an invisible bond of loyalty, which means that even now I cannot share that sentence with you. So I must ask for your forbearance and understanding in not sharing this detail.

I wonder if you think why didn't she just take a deep breath, weigh up the evidence logically, and hand the situation straight over to the medical profession? Might I have done that, if my son had had a lump on his leg? What was it about the symptom of one spoken sentence that did not concur with consensus reality that caused such a blind panic in me? Let me try to explain.

Psychosis in the Family. As I write these words they still conjure up in me a sense of horror and disbelief. Surely this is not the book I am writing? Surely this is a book for someone else to write? Can you hear my inner screams? Madness, psychosis, insanity, asylums, stigma, psychiatry. These words had been firmly locked away in the repressed and denied parts of my unconscious. They were strictly for other people, maybe even just for people in films. This was my level of denial. I felt somehow that I had been invited to appear on the Universe's version of Mastermind and I wanted to shout, "This is not my chosen subject!"

This is my story as a single, fifty-plus mother watching her beloved son suffer the agony of psychosis. This is my story as an unwilling protagonist who held her own prejudices, opinions, fears, judgement, denial, and ignorance around mental illness. I openly confess to my shame, stigma, and guilt. It still takes effort and courage for me to be totally honest without seeking to avoid all the labels. I openly confess to never being able to think of my son as anything other than just temporarily, biochemically, ill.

Of all the prejudices I held at that time there was one I find difficult to admit even now. It is this: if someone other than my son had become psychotic, one of his friends or my daughter's friends, would I have ascribed their illness to faulty genes or inadequate parenting and told myself it could never happen in my family? It would have been that joy all humans experience when they observe evils from which they are free: smug, self-satisfied superiority. I had systematically avoided any contact with what I believed to be "madness" because I did not wish to be confronted with this issue

So what exactly was I responding to on that pale grey Tuesday? Was I responding to the realization that my son had an illness? Ken Wilber, one of the most widely read and influential American philosophers of our time, in *Grace and Grit* (2001), the story of his and his wife's battle with breast cancer, defines illness as follows:

> In any disease, a person is confronted with two very different entities. One, the person is faced with the actual disease process itself— a broken bone, a case of influenza, a heart attack, a malignant tumour. Call this aspect of the disease "illness". Cancer for example, is an illness, a specific disease with medical and scientific dimensions. Illness is more or less value-free; it's not true or false, good or bad, it just is—just like a mountain isn't good or bad, it just is.
>
> But two, the person is also faced with how his or her society or culture deals with that illness—with all the judgements, fears, hopes, myths, stories, values, and meanings that a particular society hangs on each illness. Call this aspect of disease "sickness". Cancer is not only an illness, a scientific and medical phenomenon; it is also a sickness, a phenomenon loaded with cultural and social meanings. Science tells you when and how you are ill; your particular culture or subculture tells you when and how you are sick. [Wilber, 2001, p. 40]

And so, I realize now that it was not the notion of the illness or the scientific disease process of psychosis that coloured my responses. My extreme reactions were to the "sickness" of psychosis as defined by our culture. Although Wilber writes movingly about cancer and its negative connotations, I believe that there is no more condemnatory judgement by society on any sickness than that of "schizophrenia" and "psychotic disorders"; the "sickness" which implies a life sentence of psychiatric drugs, sectioning, madness, and violent crimes. Think of the headlines in the red-tops. "Paranoid Schizophrenic Murders Girl in Park." As one of my clients says, she never dares tell anyone that her brother has schizophrenia as she believes the public image is the equivalent of him being an axe-wielding murderer.

So, in that opening twenty-four hours, I was responding to the way I believed society views the "sickness" of psychosis. We live in a culture that often denies that those who suffer from psychoses are part of the human family. My fear bought into all the social and cultural conditioning I had experienced in the previous fifty years. For the truth of the matter is that I had never set foot in a psychiatric ward. I was operating from a place of ignorance and bias.

Although I had no psychiatric experience, I did have my psychotherapy training. So here goes for another confession that makes me inwardly cringe and wonder at my own levels of denial. In the June preceding that August day I had attended a series of lectures on *DSM-IV — The Diagnostic and Statistical Manual of Mental Disorders*, which is used in both America and Britain to classify the symptoms of all known mental disorders. This system enables the medical profession, the psychiatric profession, psychologists, and psychotherapists to have a single referential tool for diagnosis.

The title of the lecture on this particular day was "Schizophrenia and other psychotic disorders". I have my typed handout:

Schizophrenia and other Psychotic Disorders

> There isn't any generally agreed definition of the term "psychotic". In talking about Schizophrenia, the *DSM-IV* is referring to one or more of the following as being indicators of psychosis
>
> Delusions
> Hallucinations
> Disorganized speech

Grossly disorganized behaviour
and Catatonic behaviour. [Unpublished Lecture Notes, CCPE]

In pen, on my notes, I had neatly written "demotivated" and "with-drawn socially". I thought of my son: he was going out less, he had left his studies. No, no, said the voice in my head. This could not happen to my son. These simple and crazy thoughts belonged to me. So, three months before that August, I was able to discount and deny what was going on before my very eyes, out of ignorance, fear, and goodness only knows what else. This contributed consid-erably to my first guilt trip, which would be repeated many times.

So, although I have my typed notes, and could professionally recognize the symptoms, there is a world of difference between a clinical diagnosis of a psychotic disorder and loving someone and watching them suffer.

My son is not a clinical entity. He is a warm, sane, loving human being with a blameless illness. And so the words and their mean-ings are terribly important to me, as I tell my story because I do not want the "sickness" of psychosis to pervade our lives. It is hard enough to live with the "illness". As a result, I hardly ever use the word "schizophrenia" now. I understand it as a psychotherapist in its diagnostic definition, but even then it is a vague term. "Schizophrenia" is often defined simply as a "severe form of mental illness". The fact is, however, that "schizophrenia" is an umbrella term used to describe a group of related disorders characterized in general by disordered thinking, feelings, and behaviour. According to Pfeiffer (1987), however, "the term 'schizophrenia' is an inade-quate and misleading diagnosis. 'Disperceptions of unknown cause' is a better term" (p. 10).

Apart from my owned sensitivity, there is another reason I choose not to use the term "schizophrenia" or "schizophrenic". This is because the words themselves have so many uses and abuses in everyday language, which present yet another symptom of our cultural ignorance and fears. "Schizophrenic" is often used to describe erratic, contradictory behaviour. For example, the summer's schizophrenic weather meant in July and August I was one day wearing a Gucci sleeveless white linen top and the next a Prada puffa jacket.

"Schizophrenia" is derived from the Greek word "schizo" mean-ing "split", which is often taken to mean a split in the personality:

a kind of Dr Jekyll and Mr Hyde duality. However, it is better described as a split from consensus reality. Nevertheless, the personality split idea is a very common misperception which contributes to an even greater misunderstanding of the illness. Although it may be argued that language is performing its natural function by appropriating words for general use, it is inappropriate to misuse the clinical term of "schizophrenic" as a synonym for "contradictory".

Of course, it took me a while to reach this point of understanding, and not without making my own clumsy mistakes. As you may remember from the "Note to reader", I called my first weekend workshop "Does someone you love have schizophrenia?" After the workshop, I had some leaflets printed and took them to the first Mental Health and Spirituality Conference. I hoped to share my work with like-minded others. However, when I showed the leaflets to one of the course leaders, a past sufferer, and asked permission to put them out on the table, her nose just curled up in distaste. She turned away from me without speaking. That taught me a lot, the hard way. I never put the leaflets out. I never spoke about my work during the conference. I came home and rethought why the term "schizophrenia" might be offensive. I put my newly printed leaflets in the bin.

I then came up with the idea of calling my work simply "Psychosis in the family". The word "psychosis" is also used to describe conditions that affect the mind, in which there has been some loss of contact with reality. Hallucinations, delusions, paranoia, and disorganized thoughts and speech are symptoms of psychosis, just as they are symptoms of "schizophrenia". So, in a way, the term "psychotic disorders", and "schizophrenia" are interchangeable in terms of being overall generic words to cover this cluster of symptoms.

However, there is a subtle difference in the cultural associations of the words. "Psychosis" is recognized as a transient condition. People can have episodes of psychotic behaviour. They are not psychotic twenty-four-seven. The experience of psychosis varies greatly from person to person, and individuals experiencing psychosis might have very different symptoms. Thus, the words "psychosis" and "psychotic disorders" carry culturally a more temporary, individual description of the problem than the heavy cultural sentence of the word "schizophrenia".

Although a person may be "psychotic", it is not the same as the label of "schizophrenic". We say "he is schizophrenic". We do not say he is a person who is schizophrenic. "Schizophrenic" is a short-hand word invented by society which leaves out the word "person". The term "schizophrenic", by definition, then robs the person of their individuality and their humanness and is an ever present indicator of the prejudiced times we still live in.

I recognize, value, and use diagnoses myself as a psycho-therapist, as they are essential and helpful in their correct clinical context. However, outside that environment, they might in fact do harm. Diagnoses focus on the pathology, on the negative. They imply that there is such a thing as a "mental disorder". They label people. They give a superficial view of a complex individual per-son. They imply, incorrectly, that people with the same diagnoses are similar in other ways. They can squeeze people into boxes that do not fit.

These, of course, are not new concepts. R. D. Laing, in *The Divided Self*, wrote:

> How can one demonstrate the general human relevance and signifi-cance of the patient's condition if the words one has to use are specifically designed to isolate and circumscribe the meaning of the patient's life to a particular clinical entity? [Laing, 1959, p. 18]

However, since Laing wrote these words there has been a new emergence of popular slang culture in relation to mental health. Terms like *maniac, psycho, schizo, paranoid,* and *wacko* are all exam-ples of derogatory labels now widely used in general speech. Day (2002) wrote in *The Mind Game* that so

> entrenched has the popular view of psychiatry become in our soci-ety today, most believe that anyone who is mentally troubled, depressed, hyperactive or exhibits eccentric behaviour of any kind is in fact sick in the head. [p. 213]

Perhaps we need seriously to question where the sickness in our society lies. My writing, therefore, seeks an orientation that does not pathologize or label. In adopting this stance, it is not, I hasten to add, my intention to minimize the very real problems the symp-toms present.

Psychosis, like any other illness, is a blameless illness. However, it is a guilt-ridden sickness in the hands of the society in which we live. One of the contributory factors is that the less the medical profession understands about the causes of an "illness", the more likely it is to become a "sickness". As yet, there is no real known cause or cure for psychosis, so society fills in the information gaps with judgements and meanings. This "sickness", then, is attributed to a personality defect, a moral infirmity, or even a sickness of the soul.

Our society uses our normal waking consciousness state as the benchmark for all of their judgements and condemnations of mental illness. Our normal consciousness, the normal beta wave state, is what we take for granted without the majority of us ever realizing how it works. Our pursuits of recreational drugs and alcohol are examples of us trying to sidestep this normal consciousness as we strive for altered states of consciousness. As T. S. Eliot says, we "cannot bear very much reality" (1935).

An "altered state of consciousness" is any state which is significantly different from normal waking consciousness. The term "altered state of consciousness" was coined in the 1970s by Carlos Castaneda. The word "state" means a momentary picture of an evolving process. Altered states of consciousness are almost always temporary. They can be induced accidentally through fever, sleep deprivation, starvation, or lack of oxygen. Intentionally, they can sometimes be reached through mind control techniques such as hypnosis, meditation, or chanting. In Western cultures, altered states are frequently attained through the use of alcohol and a variety of recreational and prescription drugs. Naturally occurring altered states of consciousness include dreams, ecstasy, and psychosis.

Psychosis, in this context, is, therefore, just one part of a spectrum of altered states of consciousness which we all experience. At one end of the spectrum is conscious meditation and awareness, and at the other end is psychosis; an "extreme state" where there is literally no control. "Extreme states", as defined by Arnold Mindell, refers to the frequency with which these states are met, not the severity of the state (Mindell, 1991, p. 13). All definitions of "psychosis" emphasize the individual's loss of control in discriminating between subjective experiences and the world of consensus reality. This loss of control is the defining factor in the illness. Psychosis may, therefore, be defined as an "altered state of consciousness" not under conscious control.

In *The Wounded Storyteller* (1995), Frank points out that "People define themselves in terms of their body's varying capacity for control . . . disease itself is a loss of predictability . . . Illness is about learning to live with lost control" (p. 30). In cancer, for instance, the carcinogenic cells are out of control. As yet, we do not truly know how to control them. The loss of control of the conscious mind in psychosis is synonymous with the loss of control that is symptomatic of all illnesses.

The illness of "psychosis" may, therefore, be redefined as a human experience, which involves the naturally occurring phenomenon of an altered state of consciousness not under conscious control. This definition allows us to understand how the symptoms of psychosis have accompanied mankind through its history, affecting 1% of the population worldwide; symptoms which do not discriminate between race, class, and geographic location. It is simply one aspect of being human.

For us to understand our loved ones and the illness, it is important to recognize what we have in common with people in "psychosis" and, indeed, the entire human race. By recognizing our commonality, we can begin to take the first step in not excluding them, not marking them as different. Different is not so very far from meaning inferior, dangerous and, by definition, not human. It is time for us to question our own attitudes and to look at our own responses of fear, mistrust, and hostility.

At the same time we have to acknowledge that extreme psychotic behaviour frightens us. I talk here from experience; this is not a theoretical discourse. At the same time, how terrifying must it be for someone to lose conscious control of their mind to the extent that they do crazy things? Extreme psychotic behaviour reminds us of our fragility and powerlessness, but so do all illnesses. Psychosis needs to be recognized as a function of being human, with all the terror, suffering, pain, and powerlessness that goes with it. Psychosis also happens to warm, sane, loving people and their families, and has done so since the beginning of time.

Of course, I knew none of this on that pale grey Tuesday. Knowing about altered states of consciousness was not how I was able to view it then. What I was responding to, of course, was the well recognized "stigma" of psychosis and mental illness in general, where an individual and even the family is disqualified from full social acceptance.

My story is therefore dedicated to giving a voice to those individuals and families who have shared my experiences and to the "wise", the second set of people whose working situation or place in society has given them insight and understanding that "psychosis" is a natural phenomenon of being human. "Wise persons" are the people before whom the individual and their families need feel no shame (Goffman, 1963, p. 41).

I hope, in the telling of my story of psychosis in the family, that I need feel no shame.

CHAPTER TWO

Living in the shadows

Diary extract

So, here is the second diary extract of the story I do not want to tell; the tale of a mother standing by, watching my young adult son with all his life before him, including a glittering career in academia, change personality from a warm, funny, loving young man to an angry and deluded person I could not relate to. In the shadowy domain we now inhabited, uncertainty and unpredictable behaviour with no basis in reality became our *modus operandi*. Relating, the fundamental aspect of human nature, was denied to us both.

I notice how resistant I am to going back and describing those dark grey days. I did not count the days or the weeks or months. I do not even know if I can put them in order now. It seems, retrospectively, to have been so much easier to tell you in electrifying detail what happened on that first day when the psychosis became apparent, when my perceptions were sharp and focused. For, ironically, what happened after that was that each nightmare day rolled into the next. My thoughts and feelings followed suit, and numbed and dumbed down to deal with the new extremes in my life.

Each day possessed a sameness of quality to it, characterized by watching my son suffering, as well as living under the ever-present threat of wondering whether he might become a danger to himself or others. That in turn brought up the fear of him being sectioned, and all the imagined horrors that might bring in its wake. As things were, he did not meet any of those criteria. As the main presenting symptom of his illness was that he himself had no insight into his symptoms, we fell outside any conventional psychiatric or medical help. Therefore, the onus fell on me to carry the symptoms.

When the burden felt too great, in desperation, I would ring a mental health charity. The advice was always the same; I had to wait until he got worse, until he was a danger to himself and others. I rang social services, and the advice was the same. So I soldiered on from necessity, registering all the different symptoms of the illness on my own. I was, in effect, running my own private, guidance free, mental health hospital for one. As ever, I was constantly looking for alternative and holistic treatments. I arranged twice-weekly private therapy and nutritional supplements for my son and changed his diet. But this is an important aspect of our story, which I will address in detail in the next chapter.

As I fell outside the mainstream conventional crisis management, mental health care system, I simply did not know who to talk to about "it". Who could I open up to? Crazily, I could not discuss it with the person it concerned most, my son, because he had no awareness of his condition. If the mental health charities could not help, where could I turn? Even in psychotherapy circles, psychosis was strictly the province of psychiatrists.

As an only child, my widowed mother, living in the North, was certainly the last person I could turn to. She was, as ever, immersed in her own sea of narcissistic depression and only saw things from her own point of view. My daughter was travelling, and my ex-husband lived in another part of the country. I somehow felt unable to share with my closest family the enormity and horror of the nature of the psychosis, as I felt a loyalty to my son's process and an unwillingness to criticize him or denigrate his experiences.

With my friends and colleagues, and initially even with my own therapist, I found myself not wanting to talk about "it". And that is exactly how I handled "it" initially. I did not name "it". I spoke in hushed tones to a select few about my son having had a nervous breakdown while doing his PhD. This sentence seemed to me to tell people that he was clever and bright and it was only a temporary, almost normal, setback for a student. That was how I dealt with "it". It was simply that I ("I" being the self image I had of myself at the time) as the mother of successful, sane, and socially conforming young adult children, could not come to terms with "it". Yet "it" became my constant, invisible companion.

Months passed before I could even recognize "it", so subtle and all pervading was its power. "It" had me totally in its grasp to the point where I did not know how to talk honestly to myself, let alone to others. "It" was my shame, my inner state of imagined disgrace, which stopped me from ever being real or authentic. Nobody saw my distraught helpless self. I covered "it" up. I didn't even cry. And so, in this diary, my challenge is to tell you, without shame, the context and content of our lives at this time and expose with self-compassion my often crazy, inadequate, and flawed responses.

Several months before the day psychosis made itself apparent, my son had come home temporarily to stay with me. The lease on his shared flat had expired and his long-term flatmates were all going their separate ways. He was doing his PhD at a London college and was unsure how to proceed financially. A couple of months earlier, he had announced that he had decided, with his professor, to leave his studies temporarily while he reformulated the exact nature of his thesis. Not someone to be questioned closely myself, I accepted this. As he is a naturally studious young man, and was still going out to libraries and galleries, I assumed he was still studying and deciding what direction his thesis would take. Another mitigating factor was that he had suffered from glandular fever after his finals. He had consistently been battling fatigue from that time. I had made up a story that he was so successful at such a young age that he was burnt-out and needed some quiet time.

I, too, was in the middle of a career change, from an interior designer to an internal designer of quite another kind. I was in the third year of a five-year transpersonal psychotherapy training course. I was engaged in a balancing act between working less and earning less and living on a financial roller-coaster. I had just sold my house to pay for the last two years of my training. I then moved into a rented flat and my son said he would come with me temp-orarily. My personal fantasy had been that I would live as an impoverished student for the next two years, studying psycho-therapy but finding my spiritual way home. God help me, but I thought I had my life sorted.

My son and I had settled into what I thought was a quiet, intro-spective way of life. I was studying avidly and in the middle of my third-year essay on the role of the unconscious in different therapy approaches. The switch to social withdrawal and recluse mode for us both was gradual and insidious. Our lives then simply devel-oped an isolated pattern of existence that accommodated our new, unwelcome, bullying guest: a guest who lay ominously poised in the shadows; a guest who decided when they would arrive, unan-nounced, and with no decency or respect for the conventional rules of humanity or society.

I strove desperately to maintain some kind of normality, but the reality was that my son was suffering from psychosis. Every time he went out of the door I made habitual catastrophic interpreta-tions, and imagined the most horrific outcomes, none of which ever came to pass, but none the less were exhausting and terrifying.

On an everyday basis, I had to observe his change in personal-ity. I had been plunged from operating in a world of consensus reality into dealing with altered and extreme states of conscious-ness. It was like living in a dark cave where the sunlight could not pierce into its long dark shadows.

From the vantage point of today, I wonder when and how I started to assimilate the fact that my son was suffering from a psychotic episode. Then I only knew the words "paranoid schizo-phrenia", and this phrase filled me with mortal terror. What did it mean for him and me? How could I ever begin to accept it? I had no choice but to adapt, but my adaptation strategy was never thought through. I could not make sense of my own experiences, so, if in the writing it seems that I did, it was not the way it unfolded at the time. My short-term action plan, if there had been one, would have been to get through each day. My long-term action plan was my grim determination to save my son from a life sentence of mental illness and medication. But I did not recognize either as such at the time. I never fully took stock; I just kept blindly going on.

In my world, I became like his shadow, secretly trailing him from the moment he got up. My days went something like this.

Woke up. Felt heavy and dark. Got up. Made tea, any tea. It didn't matter which kind, it all tasted the same. Ran bath. Got into bath. Didn't appreciate soothing warm water, it was only a bath. Washed hair. Dried hair. It was clean. I was presentable. Got dressed. Didn't care what I wore. Put on make-up. Ate breakfast. Anything. Didn't care what it tasted like.

When I looked in the mirror, I did not recognize the dark shadows under my eyes as an ever-present indicator of my harrowed existence. Apathy and disinterest in everyday matters was my new way of being. I was waiting for his late morning to start, so that I could assess how he would be that day.

The day starts. He is up. He is having tea and breakfast. Nothing odd to report. Breathe inward sigh of relief. Nothing untoward, thanks be to God. Relax and breathe out for five minutes. He goes back into his room. Is he depressed or very depressed? Is he angry? Is he deluded? At least I know he is in his room and it is quiet. Maybe he will be OK today; he seemed fine at breakfast. Maybe he is studying or reading. My mind is never still. I am constantly shadowing his state of mind. The fact that my own mind was such a mess did not occur to me.

I was continually watching and listening for signs of impending psychosis; I was also looking for and exaggerating signs of normality as evidence of the psychosis departing. It was like walking on eggshells. The truth of the matter was that I never knew what was going on in his mind. But it would be some time before I reached the realization that we never know what is going on in someone else's mind, psychotic or not. I had a lot to learn about human behaviour, especially my own.

Around this time, I had a dream. I dreamt I had literally fallen off the edge of the world. I found myself on a strip of land where the people were half elephant and half man. Even in the dream I felt totally lost and bewildered as I tried to adjust to a world I could not make sense of.

At my college, being with other transpersonal therapists, I knew others would be able to empathize with my broken heart, but even so I felt that on some level they turned away, not from unwillingness, but from bewilderment at the mention of psychosis and no shared experience. I could think of no way to alleviate my leper-like feelings. Day after day, people would say, "I don't know what to say." I felt totally alone and silently pitied.

In this place of extreme isolation, I was besieged by feelings of inadequacy in the face of my son's illness. What had caused it? Was it a genetic inheritance from the violent father I never knew? Was it, God forbid, my own poor mothering? Was it a transgenerational issue? Was it due to my son's use of cannabis in his teens, exacerbated by his parents divorce? My mind was in turmoil as I pondered all these hideous possibilities. I felt overwhelmed by the darkness and despair of mental illness, compounded by the darkness and despair of my guilt and shame. I pounded my pillow with anger as I railed at God for doing this to my son and me. Through my therapy training, on very rare occasions I was paradoxically able to wonder if I could find meaning in the experience, but somehow I felt that this was a grandiose reaction to my intense pain. Solace and peace and surrender seemed beyond my grasp.

My world had gone mad. My son had retreated into the shadowlands of his unconscious world and I had become a shadow of my former self.

Reflections on living in the shadows

My diary deals in the main with my emotional responses to the presenting symptoms of my son's illness. Actually, change that: not one of them was a response. To respond means to act with an awareness of choice. What I experienced were blind reactions over which I had no control whatsoever.

My reactions were, of course, coloured by the context of our lives at the time. It needs to be taken as read, at this point, that the same contextual circumstances never occur for any one individual's experience. My reactions were simply my reactions, and these, of course, were linked to and influenced by my previous experiences and behaviour patterns. So, my story is, by necessity, coloured by both the context of our lives and my own behavioural patterns. If it sounds clear now, it is only with hindsight that I can make these observations.

At that time I was, mercifully, working from home. I worked one or two days a week as an interior designer and the rest of the time was devoted to my therapy training, which consisted of seeing clients, going for therapy, and attending supervision, lectures, and experiential weekends. In retrospect, what interests me is the strange echo from the past that motivated me, at age fifty, to change my career path to become a transpersonal/spiritual psychotherapist.

Sixteen years before, I had read *The Road Less Travelled: The New Psychology of Love, Traditional Values and Spiritual Growth* by M. Scott Peck (1983). We were on holiday in Barbados. I was a tanned, slim, thirty-four-year-old, bikini-clad woman with, seemingly, everything. My children splashed happily in the azure blue swimming pool, my husband sat in the shade sipping his rum punch. I remember distinctly finishing what by now was a very sun-curled paperback. I remember a far-away look coming into my eyes. I was inspired by Scott Peck's idea that, through psychotherapy, we could understand our problems and difficulties as opportunities for spiritual growth. I remember thinking that what I really wanted to do with my life was to become a spiritual psychotherapist. Perchance to dream, but the intention was set. The universe heard my request and rolled into action. Sixteen years later, I moved from the northern grey skies of Yorkshire to London and, as a menopausal fifty-year-old single mother, enrolled for my formal training.

Is it really true that the book that first inspired me to change my career was now full of quotes seemingly directly aimed at the context of my life's problems? Quotes that dignified mental illness and its suffering.

> This tendency to avoid problems and the emotional suffering inherent in them is the primary basis of all human mental illness. Since most of us have this tendency to a greater or lesser degree, most of us are mentally ill to a greater or lesser degree, lacking complete mental health. [Peck, 1983, pp. 14–15]

> that the unpleasant symptoms of mental illness serve to notify people that they have taken the wrong path, that their spirits are not growing and are in grave jeopardy. [Peck, 1983, p. 311]

Did these words imprint themselves in my unconscious, somehow just waiting for these dark days to carry me forward to the place where I would come face to face with so-called mental illness?

Words that would inspire me to question both the very concept of mental health and mental health problems and encourage me to look beyond the present widely accepted medical model of psychosis.

I had always been someone who had quested for meaning in what seemed to me to be a very random existence. When I enrolled for my formal psychotherapy training and had to say a few words about myself, I described myself not as a professional interior designer, but as a spiritual workshop junkie. I had been, as the television series describes it, "Desperately Seeking Something". I had studied shamanism, Feng Shui, and the I Ching, spiritual healing, colour therapy; you name it, I had done it. I had not known what I was looking for and I certainly did not find it, even though the answers were inherent in all the disciplines.

Within a few weeks of beginning my training, I realized I had been on what is termed a spiritual bypass! My path of study through the spiritual disciplines had provided an entrancing journey into the esoteric without my ever having to stop and address the basic questions of who I was or why I behaved as I did. But now my psycho-spiritual journey and training had begun in earnest, including personal therapy. I had at last begun to traverse the hidden depths of my inner psyche. As Carl Jung so succinctly pointed out, those of us who look outside dream, while those who look inside awaken. I was in a process of constant self-examination and starting to take some sort of personal responsibility for my responses. I began to embark on a transition from my world of earthly and material values to a place where I was able to consider what was really important to me. I realized that everything was a matter of perception and every idea had its counterpart. I learnt how I had been injected with beliefs from my parents and was unconsciously living my life from the learned and adapted personality.

Just when I thought I was about to begin a more fulfilling life, and gain some sort of spiritual marks from the universe for all my four years of intensive personal work, I found myself in the darkest place I had ever been. There was not one single aspect of my life I felt good about. The words of my college director kept ringing in my ears, "It is not the problem itself that is the problem; it is how we choose to respond to it." I felt as if responding to my son's illness was an insurmountable problem; this was a bridge too far. But, nevertheless, my training and his words were all I had to keep me going.

Nothing, not my fifty years' life experience, the training, or the spiritual bypass prepared me in any way for the reality of living with psychosis on a daily basis. For living with someone in psychosis means that they see the world outside as symbols of their inner worlds, as their own creation, including their fears and desires. All of us do the same when we dream. In dreams we produce events, we stage dramas, which are the expression of our unconscious. While we are asleep we are convinced that the product of the dreams is as real as the reality that we perceive in our waking state. We believe in the reality of our dreams while we are having them, as unquestioningly as someone in a psychotic phase believes in their reality. Not only does someone in psychosis fully engage with their personal reality (I prefer to call it that rather than a delusion or hallucination), they have no insight into it as outside consensus reality. They also hold compelling subjective convictions about it that are not susceptible to contrary experience or to counterargument.

The experiences of two clients, who expressed their despair in therapy over their attempts to negotiate the compelling subjective convictions of their adult children, serve to illustrate this point.

John is a highly educated, intellectual, middle-aged, professional man. He is in despair about his daughter, Angela. Angela, twenty-seven, had suffered several psychotic episodes with intermittent hospital stays.

The previous weekend, Angela had visited her parents at home. She was in an acute state of anxiety. Angela believed that aliens had implanted a device into her brain which would enable them to suck her off the planet. John spent several hours trying to reason with her. He told her that aliens were the stuff of TV and sci-fi films. He was exhausted from trying to put his daughter's mind at rest. At the same time, he could see how much his daughter was suffering. Angela would not be pacified, and begged him to take her to hospital to have the implant removed.

John managed to contact her psychiatrist and arranged for her to be taken in the next day. Angela's conviction and anxiety were so compelling, that the psychiatrist arranged for her to have a brain scan almost immediately. Of course, the scan showed no evidence of an implant. The psychiatrist, and by now the entire ward staff, endlessly tried to reassure her that there was no implant by showing her the strong visual evidence of the implant-free scan.

Angela was not pacified by the evidence one iota. She remained convinced that they had just not managed to spot the implant and still clung to the belief and the fear that she would be sucked off the planet. She remained in a high state of anxiety until the medication began to have effect.

This illustrates how the beliefs in psychosis are not subject to counter-evidence even when supported by professional visual evidence. The above example is perhaps indicative of how the outside world perceives the reality of the psychotic person living in a world of aliens. But there are many more subtle alterations to reality that occur on an often daily basis.

The following is probably a more mundane and common example. Note that, as ever, life, even in psychosis, often centres around the business of everyday living, food, money, alcohol, etc., rather than the heavily publicized, more extreme delusions of aliens and implants.

Marjorie is a glamorous, intelligent, middle-aged woman. Her twenty-nine-year-old son, Martin, has been having psychotic episodes for the last twelve years. He is presently on medication. He lives in a flat in her neighbourhood. She gives him a weekly allowance, which she has tried various ways of paying but, whatever method she uses, he cannot manage. She oversees his needs and general well being together with his community psychiatric nurse.

She tells me she is worn to a frazzle each weekend with repeated phone calls from her son asking for money. Her fear is that if she gives in to his financial demands she is funding him to buy cannabis and alcohol, which cause his condition to deteriorate. Here is a typical telephone conversation between them.

Martin: Mum, you know how the Mafia works and what is going on. I need some cash for tonight, I haven't got any food.

Mum: You have already had your allowance for the week.

Martin: You know what is going on. I need some food.

Mum: I will call at the supermarket and bring you some food and fags round later.

Martin: You know that isn't what the Mafia wants. I need the cash now.

The Mafia certainly figure in Martin's altered states of reality. Martin makes generalized assumptions that his mother understands these altered states. Marjorie cannot determine, however, whether her son is now using the threat of the "Mafia" to his own advantage to get money. She is confused about where the lines of reality are being drawn. She feels defeated before she begins. His assumptions are that she fully understands his reality. She neither wants to challenge him nor collude with him.

I, too, found dealing with altered states the most profoundly unnerving experience. Feelings of sheer futility overwhelmed me, as I was stripped of logic and a shared language for daily life. Psychotic episodes seemed to automatically preclude humour, affection, connection, and touch. These were now merely words from the past.

I, of course, was convinced that my reality was the benchmark that we should adhere to. But, at the same time, I began to realize that psychosis is unique as an illness because it not only invites us, but forces us, willing or not, to look beyond the world we can see to the dreaming world, and the unconscious mental processes of our mostly hidden mind. In psychotic behaviour, the unconscious processes of unreason are brought into waking reality, for all to see and to witness. Psychosis simply does not allow us to remain in the world of logic and reason and consensus reality.

However, I am all too aware that, as intelligent people, most of us are as oblivious to the workings of our mind as we are about the internal workings of the engines in our cars. In the same way as we drive around taking our cars for granted, so we can go through life without needing or bothering to find out how our minds work. Just as when the car breaks down is possibly the only time we might think of looking under the bonnet, so it is with mental health problems: often it is only when we are psychologically distressed or a witness to it, that we question the workings of the human mind.

Many so-called drivers are blessed by ignorance and simply seem to enjoy the jolly ride of life itself. But that was not how it was for me. I was most certainly not enjoying the ride of life. I felt I was no longer in the driving seat. If I drew the analogy of psychosis as being a failure of the engine of the mind, it was devastating to consider that there seemed to be no garages or mechanics that had ever come up with root causes, or an agreed repair programme of assured success.

Had there been a guaranteed psychosis success programme would I have felt driven to understand the mind? Perhaps not, but I was already firmly on this track through my studies. I had come to believe passionately that understanding ourselves is crucial to our psychological well being, mental health problems or not. I totally agree with Sarno (1998) who wrote that:

> Someday we will realize that the study of our personalities is more important than reading, writing and arithmetic. It will be part of basic education to know about the unconscious and repression, most particularly about what each of us is keeping in check. [p. 162]

What is extraordinary is that, at the precise time my world caved in, I had already started writing about what motivates human behaviour. Only three weeks before our unwelcome, bullying guest arrived, I had written in the opening sentence of an essay: "It is the study of human nature itself that is Freud's unique and pioneering contribution to the field of psychotherapy."

I still find these words inspiring. Psychotherapy: the study of human nature itself. It really should read Psychotherapy: the study of human nature through self-awareness. In this context, psychotherapy offers the tantalizing possibility of becoming aware of what makes us do the things we do not want to do, and not do the things we do want to do. It offers a path towards leading a more fulfilling and satisfying life. In general, psychotherapy does not seem to get that good a press. Perhaps this is because the treatment aspects of psychotherapy tend to overshadow its premise as a basic study of human nature. The public perception of psychotherapy as a treatment is often a caricature of a "shrink" offering the talking cure to some gullible, friendless person. But psychotherapy has more to offer than just a "talking cure". It offers insight into what motivates human behaviour, which takes me back to the opening sentences of my essay:

From his earliest days Freud observed that clients presented, frequently feeling not in conscious control of themselves. It was Freud's unique contribution to show that the psychological symptoms of distress did not respond to reason or reassurance. From this Freud realised that human behaviour is often governed by the unconscious and not the conscious mind. Psychological symptoms had to be understood as the products of unconscious motives and feelings.

This is what Freud gave us, the insight that how we see the world is through a marriage of conscious and unconscious processes. Imagine now a large circle, and then draw a tiny niche in it. That niche represents your conscious mind and the rest of the circle, say 95%, represents your unconscious (Peck, 1983, p. 260). Your conscious mind—that giver of logic and reason that you believe you can rely on nearly all the time—is tiny in proportion to the unconscious.

The fact of the matter is that "Virtually every aspect of mental life is connected in some way with mental events and processes that occur below the threshold of awareness" (Tallis, 2002, p. 182). It is now widely recognized that, without a thorough understanding of unconscious processes in the brain, we will never have a thorough understanding of mental health and the psychological symptoms of mental health problems. Put another way, the unconscious mind rules. The unconscious mind resides below the surface. It is the possessor of extraordinary knowledge that happens outside of our awareness. It knows more than we know, the "we" being defined as our conscious self.

Freud also went further,

He suggested that our most valued characteristics - free will, rationality and a sense of self - are mere illusions, and that we are all the products of unconscious and uncontrollable forces in the mind. [*ibid.*, p. xi]

In psychosis, the person loses free will, rationality, and a sense of self. The person is acting from unconscious and uncontrollable forces in their mind. And, this is the rub, so are we.

So, how do these unconscious and uncontrollable forces in our minds work? In the first place, we live in large part on the basis of habit. As Bateson (1972) points out "Habit is a major economy of conscious thought" (p. 141). We can do things without consciously thinking about them. We have all driven long distances and arrived at our destination realizing that for a large part of the journey, our mind has been preoccupied on several topics of concern. Our automatic pilot, the unconscious, has driven us there, yet we do not understand or have any control over these processes. It is not as if we decide to let the automatic pilot take over; the gear shift itself, from conscious to unconscious, is also unconscious.

> Samuel Butler was perhaps the first to point out that, that which we know best is that of which we are least conscious, i.e., that the process of habit formation is a sinking of knowledge down to less conscious and more archaic levels. [*ibid.*]

Dreams are often described as the royal road to understanding the unconscious. It is through dreams that even the most disciplined and ordered conscious mind can begin to understand the limitless, frenetic, wild adventures that lie in the unconscious. The unconscious reveals itself in its full glory in dreams; its activity, in relation to its many parts and selves, extends far beyond the cultural and sociological conditions of our lives. Psychosis also reveals the unconscious, but not in its full glory. It is uncontained and spills over into waking reality with the unchallengeable conviction that this is reality.

Just as psychosis does not respond to reason or reassurance, other day to day psychological disturbances, such as mild depression, workaholism, and retail therapy addiction, do not respond to reason or logic. Problems of the conscious mind are often not solved by the conscious mind.

Unknowingly, at the time, I was keeping myself busy avidly reading and researching human behaviour as a key strategy in my survival. And then one day I found it, the quote I had been unconsciously looking for:

> Freud noted, however, that psychosis is not restricted to those labelled mentally ill: *[E]ach one of us behaves in some respect like a paranoic, corrects some aspect of the world which is unbearable to him by the construction of a wish and introduces this delusion into reality.* [Mollon, 2000, p. 48]

Somehow I felt heartened, not saddened, by these words. This was Freud, the grandfather of psychotherapy, speaking: *"Psychosis is not restricted to those labelled mentally ill"*. For the human condition is that "we can face deep anxieties or conflicts for only so long. The mind has ways of evading such things" (Hobson, 2002, p. 151). We all employ unconscious defence mechanisms to shut the things out of consciousness that we do not want to face, or that do not fit in with our self image. The pain of the wife of the successful businessman who has a mistress is so unbearable she puts it to one side as she hosts her Saturday evening dinner party as the perfect wife with her perfect husband. She constructs her wish, her delusion, that all is well, and acts it out, into reality. We all do it all the time. These are how our defence mechanisms work.

Maybe it is a defence against my own reality that enables me to find some solace in the idea that psychosis is a normal and natural, if extreme, aspect of the interface between conscious and unconscious mental processes. As Winnicott (1965, p. 73) states, "By the term psychosis I refer to a deeper line of defence", beyond the usual defence mechanisms we all use.

Just as if someone had unpicked one tiny cotton thread of a large bedspread, I began to feel the most minute and fleeting respite from the unremitting curse of madness and insanity. In the shadowlands between the interactions of the conscious and unconscious mind might lie a slender gossamer thread of hope. In the dark shadows of my cave of despair, I clung to it like a baby.

CHAPTER THREE

Disorder, disorder

Diary extract

Nightmares unfold in different ways. My nightmare continued, but unfolded in bizarre and unforeseen ways, just like real nightmares do. There were twists and turns in events that I thought would help which were now causing me extra anxiety. Could I become any more anxious? I did not know which was worse; the hellish reality of my life as it was, or worrying about what other demons might appear over the horizon. Both kept me firmly from smiling about anything.

Having read somewhere that a positive family atmosphere is an important aspect of recovery from psychosis, I decided to ask my daughter and her boyfriend to return from their overseas travels. Hopefully, having more people around doing normal things would help. They were going to arrive in a few weeks and I just had to move out of my rented two-bed student garret. I needed to find a three-bedroomed house and fast. I didn't know how I was going to achieve it, but it just felt like small potatoes compared with trying to get my son back to health.

Healing for my son was my absolute main priority. He still remained outside any conventional medical care as he was neither violent nor a danger to himself. He somehow realized he was not well, but had no insight into the likely psychiatric diagnosis relating to his symptoms. It was all made more complex by the post-viral fatigue and aftermath of the glandular fever, which I believed was still significantly affecting him. When I felt particularly over-wrought, I would still telephone various mental health helplines, hoping to hear a different message to the "wait for disaster to strike" one. It was really crazy. But I was no longer a judge of what was crazy and what was not. In truth, I could hardly distinguish between the days when I was overwrought or particularly overwrought.

While the work of R. D. Laing resided only in some dim recess of my mind, I had, on the very first day of my son's illness, been given the contact details of a psychotherapist who had trained with him. Somewhere, somehow, I had come to associate Laing with the term "anti-psychiatry", and knew that he held a compassionate and radically different view of insanity. While psychosis is not the province of general psychotherapy, I knew that the recommended psychotherapist worked with psychotic states, which was music to my ears. Without bothering to indulge in my usual round of research, I suggested to my son that he might like to go for therapy with this unknown person. Perhaps it was because I was a therapist that he so readily agreed. And that was that, from the very begin-ning he went for regular sessions each week. I was going religiously to my own therapy; it was just how our life was.

It is interesting, as the story unfolds, to notice what my son would agree to undertake and what he would reject. It is not easy to persuade someone in an altered state to respond to reason, but all the way through he chose quite definitively what he would and would not do. These decisions were not necessarily based on logic or reason, but seemed to emanate from some innate guiding force that went beyond the illness.

So, in those early months, I was comforted by the knowledge that my son was receiving therapeutic support. His therapist also suggested that he attend private Tai Chi classes with a teacher who worked in the same building. This provided some structure to the week, albeit only for three hours. I fervently hoped that this combi-nation would yield some positive results and, in my most magical thinking episodes, I fantasized that the whole nightmare would simply end and normality would return.

The other avenue we explored was the orthomolecular approach pioneered by Carl Pfeiffer. Indeed, you will remember, it was his book, *Nutrition and Mental Illness: An Orthomolecular Approach to Balancing Body Chemistry* (1987), that my daughter bought on that first day of my son's illness. Orthomolecular medicine, conceptualized by double Nobel Laureate, Linus Pauling, is the practice of optimizing health and treating disease by providing the correct amounts of vitamins, minerals, amino acids, enzymes, essential fatty acids, and other substances which are natural to the body's environment.

Eventually, I discovered an approach called "orthomolecular psychiatry", which had been pioneered by Abram Hoffer and his colleagues way back in the 1950s and was still being practised. Hoffer's vast research identified vitamin and mineral deficiencies, heavy metal toxicity, chronic infections, and allergies among the many other things that can mimic schizophrenia.

> Dr Hoffer more closely investigated allergies among his schizophrenic patients and found that of approximately 200 patients "about 60 percent were allergic to foods and when these foods were eliminated, they improved or became normal". [Marohn, 2003, p. 71]

Not only that, but Hoffer claimed that he had treated over 4,000 acute patients since 1952 with a 90% recovery rate if the regimen was followed for at least two years (Hoffer, 1999, p. 43).

Even though there is no empirical evidence for this approach, it did not sound to me like some new-fangled, under-researched approach, and offered us some genuine hope. I soon found out that the only place in England that offered such treatments was the Institute of Optimum Nutrition, but I was more than delighted to learn that they had a nutritionist who specialized in mental health problems. As my son was able to talk openly about his digestive problems and fatigue, he seemed genuinely pleased to go along.

Prior to his first visit, I called the nutritionist to discuss the delicate nature of the referral. I needed to explain that my son, who would be attending on his own, might not be able to reveal some of his symptoms. She was extremely understanding and confirmed that this was often the case. From the very first appointment, without waiting for the allergy and neurotransmitter tests to come back, she immediately took him off junk foods that contained refined sugar as well as all white flour, gluten, and dairy products. In addition, she put him on a course of vitamin supplements and fish oils. When he did have blood tests for food intolerances, they showed that he was actually allergic to wheat, gluten, and dairy, as well as showing many food intolerances. His digestion was badly affected.

Being able to do something positive, like adjusting our diet, was enormously empowering, even in these circumstances. At least we were addressing the physical aspect of the illness in the only way we had available to us. My son fell in with the diet immediately, and actually took a healthy interest in this nutritional programme, regularly taking his vitamin supplements. He was in any case drug, alcohol, and nicotine free. I had already tested as intolerant to gluten and milk two years before, so it was not difficult to follow this regime. But these were early days for this orthomolecular approach in England, so, unlike programmes in Canada, the follow-up consultation was six weeks away. This meant we were still left alone with the huge psychological problems that confronted us on a daily basis.

I am only too aware at this point that I might sound like some New Age hippie who believes that drinking nettle tea, eating goji berries for breakfast, and saluting the sunrise will sort out the most serious of health problems. This was not how it was. I well and truly had my back against the wall. I was not eschewing conventional care. It just was not available to us until my son got worse. The dedication and personal interest I had in holistic methods was balanced by reading everything I could find on psychosis and antipsychotic medicines. I was hyper aware if anyone had any links with psychiatry. I was constantly looking out for a referral to a recommended psychiatrist. In fact, I had the number of one carefully written in my personal notebook, just waiting for the day we could use his services. I had even rung the psychiatrist's secretary to ask if I could see the psychiatrist to tell him about my son. However, she told me my son had to come of his own accord. I did not know how to get my son to go. It seemed an impossible task to initiate the words psychiatry or psychosis into the conversation.

I tried to educate myself in whichever way I could. I found, through *Rethink* (a national mental health charity), a meeting for carers of people with schizophrenia in Camden. I made a resolve to go even though it was Tuesday and I worked that day. Two lovely young girls in their twenties, who looked younger than my son, had neatly laid out on the table a selection of leaflets of what current mental health services were offering. The main attraction of the meeting for the others, it seemed to me, was the free tea and sandwiches. Half a dozen of us sat around not talking about why we were there. I did not know what to say and to whom. The therapist in me wanted to ask the other people how they felt, but it seemed that the lunch was meant to be a welcome haven rather than a self-disclosure group. I did not find the shared experiences I was looking for. My disappointed self did not have the sandwiches or the tea. I took the leaflets and smiled at everyone and slunk home.

And these were the positive, if randomly put together, steps that I took. But the reality was that our omnipresent unwelcome guest still dominated our lives. Even if there was a day off, or several hours off, its presence was always with us, either in the form of small irrational incidents or a hovering, general feeling of anxiety, dread, and uncertainty. Its presence had the ability to knock a black hole into the centre of my being and leave me reeling in despair. At the same time, in the next millisecond I would strive to normalize things, maybe even pretend it had not happened. Because that was how it was, a lot of it was quite normal, everyday stuff, punctuated by unreason. It wasn't all madness.

But there were days when I was mad, mad as a bag of snakes. One particular day, I completely overreacted. I felt as if I could no longer cope with the anxiety and the physical gnawing black hole in the pit of my stomach. My son had gone out, I had no idea where, or when he was coming back. I was feeling desperate. I felt as if I could no longer live in the void of not knowing what was going to happen. I cannot believe I am writing this, but here goes. And so, in the depths of my black hole, without any premeditated thought, I reached for my mobile and called my son's therapist, with whom I was having no contact whatsoever. I can still see where I was standing as I held the phone in my hand. I am sure the panic in my voice was evident. I introduced myself and explained that I did not know how to cope with not knowing what was going to happen next. In crisp, clear tones only fit for the Antarctic and in slowly enunciated tones for the very stupid, he reminded me that he only saw my son for two hours a week, and that his responsibility ended there.

How can I describe my reaction? If I had felt the size of a small pincushion before, I now felt less than the size of a pinhead. What was worse was that I knew he was professionally correct. It was made even more embarrassing and demeaning by the fact that I was a trainee therapist. I should never have called him; I knew that. I had completely lost my sense of what was appropriate behaviour, both professionally and personally. I felt even more alone, and began to suspect, from his extremely cold tone, that maybe the therapist thought I was part of the problem. My sense of helplessness and isolation in the unfolding twists of the nightmare increased.

I tried to think of it from other perspectives. I tried to put myself in the therapist's shoes. How would I feel, as a therapist, if one of my client's mothers called me? I would surely be shocked. But then, I did not see therapy patients who were out of touch with reality and had no insight into their condition. He was the expert; surely he must be used to these situations. I was obviously over-reacting, oh HELP, HELP, HELP! I was losing it.

But, from another perspective, I felt totally slighted and excluded from a process which I had initiated and which we as a family were funding. Of course, my timing was ill conceived and my actions entirely inappropriate. I accepted that fully at the time, as I do now. But that cold and harsh reaction to my obvious distress formed another small part of the seed that would grow into this book. For the reality was I sitting on a time bomb, waiting for my son to get worse. And what did "worse" mean for God's sake— harm to himself or harm to others? How much worse could things get?

Of course this was only one day, one frame in a very long video. The therapy continued just as if that horrendous phone call had never happened and, what is more, I really wanted it to even if I had doubts about the role I might be cast in. I was so pleased that my son had somewhere to unburden himself in whatever way was best for him. As a committed psychotherapist, I was convinced that the therapy had to be helping him.

Several weeks later there was word from the therapist. He wanted to set up a family meeting with my son, myself, and my ex-husband. His stated explanation was to clarify some facts. During the early evening meeting, the therapist stated some of our son's beliefs and asked us for verification. My son sat in silence, but in very obvious distress. The atmosphere was cold but polite. I felt critical of the therapist and his style. Where was empathy, I wanted to scream at him. Another voice in my head told me to be reasonable and accept different therapies and styles. However, I felt we were there for the therapist to be able to distinguish a sense of my son's beliefs for his own benefit. I did not have the insight to recognize that we were being scrutinized, nor did I know, then, that psychotic beliefs are not subject to counter-argument, so it could be of no value to my son. To make things even more confusing, the therapist recommended that he thought it would be better if my son did not see a psychiatrist.

We left. My son said he preferred to travel home alone. My ex-husband and I fell into the dusky reality of the busy early evening streets of London. There were no words for our experience. We had just visited psychotherapy hell. We were in some kind of horror movie with our own son. I had found the whole hour excruciatingly painful. There was no recognition from the therapist that it was difficult for my ex-husband and me. Could he not see how our hearts were broken?

But, strangely enough, I later discovered a hidden blessing. At the time of the visit I was unaware of *Sanity, Madness and the Family* (Laing & Esterson, 1964). If I had known the contents of this book I might have felt even worse, as it is based on the hypothesis that madness is a result of ugly patterns of affection, hatred, manipulation, and indifference within the family. I did not know that we were being considered as the perpetrators of our son's illness. Even more of a blessing was that, mercifully, I had no idea of the concept of the "schizophregenic" (literally, schizophrenia inducing) mother, who is often cited as the real cause of psychosis resulting from manipulative mixed messages. But in my gut I somehow knew. I felt discriminated against. My nightmare became even more unbearable. I felt I was in a double bind; I wanted the therapy to continue, but I was worried that I was being presented as the perpetrator of the problem.

And then my son announced he was going to the new local doctors' practice as the therapist had suggested that he see a neurologist to make sure he didn't have a brain lesion. I could perfectly well see the sense of this, but his therapist did not contact me or my ex-husband to voice these serious concerns; so, early one morning, my son went out to see an unknown GP at the local practice. He returned one hour later in the most agitated state I had yet witnessed. He seemed angry and deeply distressed, but at the same time refused to talk.

But, despite my distress, I wondered if this might not be a good opportunity. If I visited the new doctor perhaps I could tell him what was happening and maybe, just maybe, we could get some medical help, even if it was a disturbing referral to a neurologist. So off I went to the surgery and made an appointment to see the same doctor that very afternoon. I told the doctor that my son was suffering from a psychotic episode. He pulled up my son's notes on his computer screen. Scrutinizing them, he said he had suspected that but, without being able to verify some of the facts with a family member, he had been unable to arrive at a definite diagnosis based on the details provided by my son.

I felt vindicated. I told him I was a psychotherapist and that, through my training college, I had been recommended to a particular psychiatrist who had an interest in the transpersonal. Daringly, I suggested that if my son returned to the surgery he might, given my son's spiritual interests, consider referring him to this psychiatrist for treatment. His tone of voice changed as he brusquely informed me that all decisions and any referrals were at his discretion and his alone. The matter was strictly between him and my son. He then looked directly at the door. The consultation was over; I slunk out of the practice. I did a lot of slinking these days.

This experience triggered a memory in me. Fourteen years before, I remembered my stepfather, only fifty-nine years old, lying in bed, with hardly enough strength to move and some days not being able to hear or see. He had seen numerous doctors from our local home practice and had received various diagnoses, including flu. He had also seen three specialists under private health insurance, culminating in a home visit in which he was diagnosed as a manic–depressive. My mother was beside herself with worry, but she hung on to this ridiculous diagnosis even though the physical symptoms were overwhelming. She came from a generation of "not wanting to bother the doctors". Her helpless and hopeless attitude was so ingrained that I could not persuade her to take action.

Fortunately, we shared the same doctors' practice, so I went to visit one of our local GPs. I told the relatively young doctor, who had treated my children for measles and mumps, that I believed my stepfather was extremely ill and was manifesting symptoms that were not being recognized. I dared to suggest that he was possibly dying, and that my mother was in denial about his condition. The doctor was kind. He looked over the top of his horn-rimmed glasses, in an attempt to make eye contact, and told me that his hands were tied. He could not do anything about an extra visit, or the symptoms, until my stepfather called him out. He was very sorry, and I believed him. A week later, my stepfather fell out of bed and was unable to get up. He was taken to hospital by ambulance. Within two days he was given an emergency operation to remove a brain tumour and the oedema (fluid) which was life threatening. Three months later he was dead.

Commonsense and appeals for help seem to play no part in such events. I was a relatively young woman when I sat with the doctor and his horn-rimmed spectacles, being told, oh so kindly, how the system worked and how medical procedures were there to protect the patient. So, the events of the day did not devastate me. But memory plays an important part in creating identity. The current events, combined with the earlier vision, stir something in me as I reflect on the importance of the family in looking after the very ill. And all this caused me to remember something else.

For three years, in my early twenties, I worked as a lab technician while training in medical sciences at the Institute of Pathology in Leeds. I was a small part of a large department undertaking research into bladder cancer. We were trained in a variety of disciplines, but the one area of work I absolutely loved was the research we carried out under the supervision of the doctors and professors in the Medical School Library opposite our building.

After about a year, it became my unspoken rule that the test tubes and microscopes were for others. My place, for a large part of most days, was in the library, looking up medical research papers. I read the *Lancet* as if it were *Vogue*. By the age of twenty-one, mainly absorbed by thoughts of which discothèque I might frequent in the evening, I came to realize that the outcome of any treatment depended largely on the person (specialist) providing the treatment and their particular area of research and expertise. Of course, the Internet has made medical research so much more accessible today, but, nevertheless, this central tenet still holds true. The medical practitioner, together with their particular area of expertise and treatment, influence in no small measure the prognosis of all illnesses. I did not value it much at the time, but my research abilities were appreciated and somewhere there are several medical papers that include my name. My Professor suggested I take another 'A' level in science and begin training as a doctor, but my fear of blood and needles took over and I left for a lucrative career selling advertising in my mini-skirt and white Courrèges boots. I never realized how useful these research skills from my formative years would be when psychosis came knocking at my door.

Now I had to get on with the roller-coaster business of daily living with psychosis. At supper that evening, my son announced he did not like the doctor and would not go back. He also stated he did not want to see a neurologist. Thank goodness, I had no investment in these avenues of help, because that was that. He had made up his mind and I would not be able to persuade him otherwise.

Apart from everything else that was going on, I was under perfectly understandable but consistent pressure from my ex-husband to "Do something!" As if I could get up one morning and say to my son, "Let's nip down to the Maudsley and get some raspberry flavoured antipsychotic syrup." Then, a few spoonfuls later, I would be able to ring my ex and report that all was well again. There were so many pressures I was under. I just existed in one huge pressure cooker called *Nobody Understanding: Living With and Loving Someone With a Mental Illness They Don't Even Know They Have*.

But all this pressure galvanized me into action. Without any defined reason, or definitive experience, I became convinced that I had to find a compassionate psychiatrist. The portrayal of institutional psychiatry, so vividly enacted in films, did nothing to dampen my innate fears, but, once again, the Internet came to my rescue. As I desperately surfed around, I stumbled upon an organization called Spirit Release.

Spirit Release is based on the premise that, after a person dies, if the soul does not go to the "light" to enter the spirit world properly, it stays mentally attached to the earth plane, where, in its lost and confused state, it attaches to a person or place. In some cases of psychosis, the text informed me, the voices heard by patients might be due to attached spirits. While I was a bit lost and confused by this hypothesis myself, my attention was captured when I noticed that the organization was run by a psychiatrist in private practice who believed in complementary treatments.

I wasted no time in getting in touch with him to arrange a visit. Once there, I told this gentle, refined man my whole convoluted story and he readily agreed to see my son from his private practice. I was relieved, as this meant that he would finally receive a psychiatric assessment. While this arrangement had nothing to do with Spirit Release, I felt that my son would be more willing to attend under that banner than he would if I suggested a psychiatrist in a mental health unit. I desperately needed a qualified case manager. The situation was way beyond anything I could manage, and I felt that this man included me as an equal in the evaluation of my son's illness.

Despite all the hoo-ha with the doctor and neurologist, my son agreed to go and see this man, whom I described as a therapist I thought could help. "It's just to talk," I reassured him. After the third visit, the psychiatrist confirmed in writing that my son, in terms of conventional psychiatric diagnostics, was suffering from psychosis. He confirmed that my son was absolutely, categorically against taking any drugs. He also stated that sectioning should only be considered if all other therapies failed, and that he would monitor him over the next three months by seeing him once a week and recommending him to other therapies if necessary. At least and at last I had a proper written diagnosis from a psychiatrist to show my ex!

With some relief, I gave my entire case notes to the psychiatrist, including details of the psychotherapist, the Tai Chi instructor, and the orthomolecular treatment. I had already aired my concerns about his psychotherapist, who was now suggesting to my son that he should go away on a Buddhist retreat. I was highly sceptical about my son's capacity to manage a completely unfamiliar environment, not to mention the possible mind-altering effects of meditation.

I informed the psychotherapist that we had now approached a psychiatrist who would oversee my son's treatment. The psychiatrist emailed the therapist, confirming his position as my son's newly appointed case manager, and that he felt a stay in an unfamiliar location was contraindicated at this time. The therapist sent a reply by email which the psychiatrist forwarded to me. And there it was in black and white. The therapist had written that the main reason he had suggested the retreat was to distance him from his mother, whom he considered to be a significant contributory factor in her son's illness. Believe it or not, there was a certain relief here. I was not mad. I was seen by my son's therapist as a contributory cause, if not *the* contributory cause.

However, just when I thought we were about to move forward, another twist took place. My son refused to go back to the psychiatrist. Heaven, hell, and high water would not sway him. Out of nowhere, he just categorically refused to go. He stated he was quite happy with the therapies he was having.

So, this diary entry ends as it began, with the preferred and chosen treatment plans being Laingian psychotherapy, Tai Chi, and the orthomolecular nutrition. Our unwelcome, bullying guest of undisclosed location and questionable reality remained firmly ensconced in our midst.

There were, however, some tentative forward steps. My son's digestion was better. He had put some weight on, and looked much better. His insomnia had improved. He was looking after himself well. His disordered thinking symptoms had stopped entirely.

Unfortunately, my disordered thinking seemed to be getting worse. Despite having applied energy, money, time, diligence, and intelligence in my search to find healing for my son, I was running around in ever-decreasing circles with a background neon sign flashing, "Do not adjust your set, there is a fault in reality."

Reflections on disorder, disorder

If we are confused or worried by what we learn, we feel driven to learn more. Here was I, both confused and worried by what I had learnt; that I had to wait for the psychosis to rear its ugly head in a dangerous way before it would render my son eligible for conventional treatment. So, in some measure, my headless chicken act of constantly looking for further treatments to help my son was not the irrational response I feared.

I have defined treatments here as the application of medical care or attention to a patient. My son was outside the application of medical care, but he was getting attention in the form of psychotherapy, orthomolecular nutrition, and Tai Chi, while residing in our exclusive private mental nursing home for one, albeit run by a matron with zero experience. But it was an agonizingly lonely ride, especially trying to find complementary and alternative therapies, which was about the only thing I could do. It seemed that the words "psychiatry" and "complementary treatments" were incompatible. How could that be in the twenty-first century, when UK research shows that two thirds of the population believe that complementary medicine is as valid as conventional treatment, with £130 million a year being spent on complementary therapies (Hawkes, 2008, p. 1). Even though the Mental Health Foundation had produced a book called *Healing Minds* in 1998 (Wallcraft), which included ten recommendations for providing complementary therapies in the mental health sector, it still seemed an impossible task to find them.

I was already in a dilemma because there is a very clear difference between alternative medicine, complementary medicine, and conventional medicine. In alternative medicine, the therapies are used alone in treating a patient, and might not be based on any scientific principles recognized by the medical profession. In complementary medicine, alternative remedies may be used, but they are employed as well as, and in support of, the conventional therapeutic measures. Conventional medicine seeks to define a specific cause for a disease and its treatments are proved to be effective by evidence derived from numerous trials and research. Integrated medicine is, of course, the "holy grail". This works on the principle of treating the causes of the disease as well as the effects it may have on the patient's home environment and mood through the use of both complementary and conventional medicine.

I, of course, was forced into the position of using alternative therapy as there was no conventional medical treatment on offer to provide support. But this was Hobson's choice: what I really wanted was the integrated approach. However, I simply could not find it. All I seemed left with was a self-made contingency plan that would, hopefully, accommodate things getting worse.

My son had already passed through the "prodromal", or first, stage of psychosis. I had been in complete ignorance of the significance of the presenting symptoms of this phase, preferring on some unconscious level to ascribe them to the huge variances that exist in human behaviour, especially in student years. These primary symptoms took place over a period of several months before the psychosis became apparent. This is the typical time frame.

While I regretted deeply not recognizing, or being aware enough, of some of the pre-warning symptoms of social withdrawal, reduced concentration, depressed mood, sleep disturbance, anxiety, suspiciousness, skipping work, and general irritability, I had no time for recriminations. I did not even stop to consider how these warning symptoms should be recognized and communicated in schools, universities, and colleges, not only to the students, but also to the teachers and parents. After all schizophrenia/psychosis is a disease which often attacks the adolescent or young adult. Not only that, but it is one of the ten leading causes of life-long, disabling illness in the world (Frith & Johnstone, 2003, p. 108).

I do not think there are many people who do not know that an abnormal lump might indicate cancer, yet worldwide mental health problems are responsible for a greater burden of disease than cancer (WHO, 2002). I had never seen the above symptoms listed as a health warning for severe mental illness, so was well and truly ignorant. I firmly believed that because my son had achieved academically he could not possibly be addicted to drugs, which seemed to be the main cautionary mental health message for our era of parenthood.

But I had no time to dwell on these matters for now we were well and truly into the second phase of the illness, the "Acute Phase", in which the symptoms ironically are described as "hard to miss". I was so busy dealing with these "hard to miss symptoms" that are, of course, blindingly obvious to the people closest to the psychotic patient and, paradoxically, not apparent at all to the person themselves. The symptoms are acting out of character and subscribing to unsubstantiated beliefs and perceptions.

It just seemed to me that the conventional treatment plan, the magic panacea of antipsychotic drugs, apparently necessitated my son being sectioned. Psychiatry is a particularly confusing branch of medicine because it carries twin obligations: care for the individual patient, and the protection of society from the patient. It has always engendered fear, probably because it is the only branch of medicine that can force treatment on individuals. I did not know how to deal with the idea of this "forced treatment". It scared the hell out of me. I had a deep, inbuilt idea that somehow this "forced treatment" might be worse than the illness itself. It all seemed so far removed from our present dysfunctional existence. Nothing constituted danger yet, even though we lived on the knife-edge of the unpredictability that psychosis had introduced into our lives. What sort of lunatic position was I in? My incomprehensible crazy world seemed a sort of safe haven to the imagined option of seeing my son forcibly manhandled and drugged.

My fears, of course, were not only individual, but also social. The cultural image of a sufferer of psychosis and their carers is nearly always portrayed in a negative light. Tabloids in particular focus on cases that involve violence or violent deaths in the form of suicides or unmotivated murders. The overall impression of psychotic behaviour is that it will result in extreme danger and causes more distress than any other single condition. The fact that there are numerous literary references to troubled, difficult, gentle people, bewildered both by the world around them and by what they are experiencing within their own minds, does not alleviate these public images one iota.

Somewhere in my psyche were horrific pictures of people chained up in early lunatic asylums. I do not know whether I was ever consciously aware of the image of William Norris, found shackled in an iron cage in Bethlem in 1814 with a stout iron ring around his neck, and around his body and arms, strong iron bars. Norris became a symbol of all that was wrong with this regime, when lunatics were often seen and treated like animals. He was released after nine years, but died of TB soon afterwards. (Maybe TB is the abbreviation for Treated Barbarically.)

Somehow, there were vestiges of this memory within me. I do not think any of us do not have some haunted image associated with the concept of lunatic asylums. In the days of the asylums, a great variety of mental problems were crowded under the same roof, with over one thousand patients in some cases. Those suffering from senile dementia, or post-natal depression, mania, schizophrenia, or simply eccentricity, were huddled together with unmarried mothers and failed suicide attempts. There were no expectations of a cure, or even treatment, and there was a deliberate attempt to keep them out of sight of the general public.

In the current fashion of do-it-yourself genealogy, it can even be part of your ancestral story to trace your very own lunatic ancestors. This is because, from 1871 onwards, the Victorian census returns recorded if an individual was considered a Lunatic, Imbecile, or Idiot. There is even a book called *Basic Facts about Lunatics in England and Wales for Family Historians* (Faithfull, 2002).

This was the level of prejudice only a hundred and thirty years ago. We have, of course, moved on in our collective psyche, but there are still plenty of allusions to the people in white coats coming to get you with their supply of straitjackets. These images form the backdrop to our current mode of looking at psychosis. They are undeniably powerful images to dispense with. They are made of the stuff of raw fear that we all dread most. It is the common link of insanity that we all share in our collective unconscious.

As I consider the notion of "raw fear", my mind takes me back to thinking about my training and what constitutes the existential approach to psychotherapy and, indeed, philosophy. The existential view is that life is at times difficult and painful and is a given of human existence. It encompasses the primary fears of existence itself, the ultimate dreads we all face when we are honest enough to look beyond the trivial nature of everyday concerns.

Existential therapy addresses the four fundamental fears: death, meaning, isolation, and freedom. *Death* anxiety we all know and recognize on some level. It is a core inner conflict between accepting the inevitability of death and the wish to continue to be. Anxiety about *meaning* presents as looking for meaning and purpose in our lives. Finding our lives meaningless leaves us alienated and depressed, questioning and unfulfilled. The anxiety of *isolation* is the unbridgeable gulf between oneself and any other being. Our basic mode of being is relational, and the ultimate knowledge that we are separate, isolated, alone, and alienated from all that is, can be the most unbearable dread of all. *Freedom* of choice is an anxiety-provoking condition. Choice, by definition, invokes loss. If we choose tea, we lose the option of coffee. Through our choices, our actions, and our failures to act, we ultimately design ourselves. We are condemned to own our own freedom of choice, to be self-responsible for that which we choose to lose in our lives.

But what about the fear of losing one's mind, surely that is an existential dread too? Surely psychosis encompasses all the existential fears. It is the death of our personality, that consistent pattern of a recognizable self, it isolates us from others, it means we cannot make rational meaning out of our thoughts, it condemns us to a place where we lose the capacity to make choices in our own best interests. Loving someone who has temporarily lost their mind feeds into these same dreads, the death of the one we knew; they are isolated from our love and concerns, we cannot make meaningful relationships with them, and we cannot make choices of how to be with them. Our responses are straitjacketed, mirroring their inability to respond to us.

Maybe it was these deep dreads that made me look ahead, trying to find treatments that might avert the worst-case scenario of my son being hospitalized. Or, at least, lead us to the best-case scenario in that situation: to find the best people in the best hospital with the best treatments, whatever that situation might look like. Inevitably, treatment plans for any kind of illness, albeit physical or so-called mental, are inherently linked to knowing the aetiology of the illness. Psychosis is generally believed to have accompanied mankind through its history, yet no agreed cause has been universally acknowledged. I am well aware that the finest of minds throughout the ages, in philosophy, medicine, and neurosciences, have applied themselves to debating the causes of psychotic illnesses. I was, however, undeterred in simply trying to find out what would help my son.

So I began what felt like my mini-mouse exploration of possible causes of psychosis. I had, of course, inadvertently already begun my search through my studies. In studying Freud, in particular, I had come to realize that psychosis could be considered as a deeper form of unconscious defence than the usual defence mechanisms we all use. Although it was Pierre Janet, in the 1880s, who originally became convinced that memories and ideas outside of awareness were the ultimate cause of mental illness, it is nevertheless Freud who is usually accredited with discovering that mental illness is caused by unconscious mental forces which intrude into consciousness in a distorted form, thereby generating the patients' symptoms.

This discovery seemed to promise a new kind of psychological treatment for the mentally ill. As Freud's theories spread to America in the 1920s,

> psychoanalytic ideas became a routine feature of medical training, and the concept of getting to the unconscious root of the problem became axiomatic in the treatment of all mental illness - the goal of all psychiatrists. [Tallis, 2002, p. 88]

This, of course, was the era of the pre-medical model.

However, the advent of psychiatric drugs in the 1950s transformed the psychiatric field, shifting the causality of mental illness back to the biochemical realm. One of my therapy teachers had been a general practitioner for fifty years. She told me that when she was a medical student in the 1950s, she had worked one summer in what in those days was called the "loony bin". She related how shocking the experience was for her. In those days, relatives dumped people in there for life. She talked of the "iffy" diagnosis processes. She remembered the matron, apparently a Hattie Jacques look-alike, telling her how the introduction of Largactyl, a tranquillizer and sedative had revolutionized the "bin". Previously, they had only constraint and restraint as a method of treatment. So it was the welcome advent of drugs that heralded the beginning of the end of long-term care, or even entire lives spent in institutions, often at the behest of the family themselves.

The fact is that, as a result of the improvement to countless patients and the end of long-term incarceration for the mentally ill, antipsychotic medications now rule conventional psychiatric treatment of psychosis. Antipsychotics carry with them an unspoken but underlying slogan of "Mental disorders are brain disorders". The current established view is that schizophrenia is a brain disorder involving some kind of neurotransmitter malfunction, so drugs thought to manipulate neurotransmitter function are the prescribed course of treatment to correct a chemical imbalance.

But the legacy of the asylums still remained a *cause célèbre*, and in the 1960s and 1970s a series of scandals about the abuse of mental patients surfaced. The whole legitimacy of psychiatry was called into question. On the back of this, but separate to it, the "anti-psychiatry" movement, led by R. D. Laing, Thomas Szasz, and

Michel Foucault, was born. Thomas Szasz wrote *The Myth of Mental Illness*, in which he propounded,

> It is customary to define psychiatry as a medical speciality concerned with the study, diagnosis, and treatment of mental illness. This is a worthless and misleading definition. Mental illness is a myth. [Szasz, 1974, p. 262]

Michel Foucault wrote *Madness and Civilization: A History of Insanity in the Age of Reason* (1988).

> On Foucault's view, madness as a general phenomenon should be seen as a creditable challenge to normality, even though there are insane horrors to which normality would be a welcome relief. [Gutting, 2005, p. 71]

But out of these three it was R. D. Laing, the English psychiatrist (who never described himself as "anti-psychiatry") who became the champion for the psychotic patient. He displayed and demonstrated a rare understanding and sympathy for their condition and their oppression. In *The Divided Self*, he wrote inspiringly and with compassion, a word not often seen in the language of psychiatry:

> What is required of us? Understand him? The kernel of the schizophrenic's experience of himself must remain incomprehensible to us. As long as we are sane and he is insane, it will remain so. But comprehension as an effort to reach and grasp him, while remaining in our own world and judging him by our own categories whereby he inevitably falls short, is not what the schizophrenic either wants or requires. We have to recognise all the time his distinctiveness and differentness, his separateness and loneliness and despair. [Laing, 1959, p. 38]

The lunatic, in one fell swoop, lost his label, and was reclaimed to the common soul of humanity. Hurrah for Laing.

Not only that, but Laing wanted to know "why *are* there no real alternatives to the depersonalizing and bureaucratic protocols of hospitalization for people in acute mental and emotional turmoil?" (Burston, 1996, p. 237). His hope was that people could "put their shattered minds back together without resorting to intrusive and debilitating treatments" (Burston, 1996, p. 243). To this end, Laing and his colleagues founded the Philadelphia Association in 1965. It is still operational, and continues with its aim of challenging accepted ways of understanding and treating mental and emotional suffering through the practice of psychotherapy. Within community households, people with serious emotional difficulties live with others for substantial periods of time and try to make sense of their difficulties and achieve more productive and fulfilling lives.

R. D. Laing was a revolutionary, who quite rightly turned the psychiatric world upside down with his ability to see the psychotic patient as "simply human" and not to see everything they did as a sign of illness. However, it was the second phase of his work that caused the greatest stir, both in the psychiatric community and to the public at large. His book *Sanity, Madness and the Family* (1964), written in collaboration with Aaron Esterson, consisted of eleven case studies of families and put forward the idea that the illness of psychosis lay not within the individual, but within the family unit, i.e., the very cause of madness lay in the immediate family itself. "It extends the unintelligibility of individual behaviour to the unintelligibility of the group" (Laing & Esterson, 1964, p. 22). This was not a new theory: for example, in 1948, Frieda Fromm-Reichmann coined the phrase "schizophregenic mother" and in 1956 Bateson put forward the "double-bind" hypothesis (Frith and Johnstone, 2003, p. 111). "To put it another way, the mother is controlling the child's definitions of his own messages" (Bateson, 1972, p. 214).

Maybe it was as a result of Laing's new found compassion for the psychotic person, and the appalling previous treatment of the mentally ill, that the cry was heard and taken up far and wide. The pathology of psychosis now appeared to lie in the realms of interpersonal relationships within the immediate family of origin. In its most basic terms, psychotic behaviour in adolescents and young adults was seen as a response to repressive and rejecting parenting. This was not a theory allied to hidden forces in the unconscious; this was about the conscious mind and the role of relationship in the formation of symptoms.

Not only did the book promote the pathology of the schizophregenic family as a root cause of madness, it also sought to diminish the medical model's theory of a brain disorder through stating that

There are no pathological anatomical findings *post mortem*. There are no organic structural changes noted in the course of the "illness". There are no physiological–pathological changes that can be correlated with these illnesses. There is no general acceptance that any form of treatment is of proven value, except perhaps sustained careful interpersonal relations and tranquilization. [Laing & Esterson, 1964, p. 17]

Laing gave psychiatry compassion and wisdom in understanding the experience of the psychotic individual, decried the medical model of medication—medication and more medication—but, at the same time, labelled and damned the immediate families as being the cause. For, although there were allusions to not all families being responsible, it would prove to be a long term and enduringly hard shackle for close relatives to shake off.

In Laing, I had found at last an alternative route to sectioning and strong medications, but I now had to come to terms with being the very cause of the illness itself. Was I a cold, hostile, over-involved mother who consistently sent out double bind messages where my spoken words contradicted my actions? Surely it was me who was now in a double bind. Could I be tempted to veer towards the medical model to overcome the possibility of my own culpability? Would it be easier to go for the expert psychiatric drug-pushing option, with its reassurance that the parent was not at fault, rather than look any further.

My God, did I question my intellectual ability to reason at this time. For wherever I researched, even in the most hallowed of tomes, I found totally conflicting material. Some examples follow.

Since the earliest days of institutional psychiatry, nurses, and some-times psychiatrists, have had shrewd intuitions that, however disturbed the admitted schizophrenic patient seemed to be, he was not alone in his disturbance. Quite often experienced staff have guessed that something unusual or even crazy, has been going on in the family of the patient, and this feeling has been expressed in remarks such as "perhaps we've got the wrong one in here". [Cooper, 1967, p. 49]

We now know that schizophrenia is fundamentally a biological problem that is no different in principle from other such problems, like cancer or heart disease or diabetes. We know that schizophrenia is not caused by possession of evil spirits, or by a weak personality, or a bad mother. [Frith & Johnstone, 2003, p. 145]

Although most modern recipients of psychiatric care find that neuroleptics to some extent control their symptoms, it is doubtful whether any are cured by this kind of treatment, and a substantial minority obtain no benefit whatsoever. [Bentall, 2003, p. 499]

Natural medicine therapies offer a future in which the monikers of fear—the "S" word and "cancer of the mind"—lose their relevance and become relics of the past as schizophrenia becomes known as a treatable condition. [Marohn, 2003, p. 192]

The treatment of psychotic states over the past two hundred years is marked by an extraordinary diversity of methods sometimes based on a theory, sometimes on analogies and single observations and sometimes on no more than doctors' or healers' instincts. People with schizophrenia and other psychotic states similar to it have been placed under extreme physical stress, exposed to exclusively psychoanalytic approaches, made comatose, injected with substances that produced fits, given electro-convulsive therapy, forced to take medications, isolated from people and all other stimuli, and given acupuncture and unusual diets. [Johannessen, Martindale, & Cullberg, 2006, p. xvii]

What started off as a search for treatments has led to me to question my own ability to reason my way through the extraordinary diversity of opinions and conflicting viewpoints on the causes of psychosis. At the core, there seems to be an ongoing debate of whether the mind is in the brain. Perhaps it is a good thing I am so confused. As I stated at the beginning of the chapter, when we feel confused or unhappy with what we learn, we feel driven to learn more.

I was driven. Maybe it had something to do with me being a Yorkshire lass that drew me to a Yorkshire lad for some plain speaking that would cut through some of the predominating theories and tell a similar story to my own. In *Untold Stories*, Alan Bennett writes movingly about his mother's mental illness. He points out that Laing and his followers seldom discussed the profoundly distressing effects that a severe mental illness had on the rest of the family, in this case his father. He points to the central tenet of their theories, that mental illness was generally the work and the fault of the family and then he writes:

> But nothing that I read or saw at that time resembled the situation in our family, the sudden defection of a loved one, her normal personality wiped out with a total loss of nerve. In Laing and Szasz the love that was on offer in the family was generally seen as rigid and repressive, with affection bartered for good behaviour. This didn't seem to me to have much to do with my father's affection for my mother, which, while not denying her faults, seemed as near selfless as one could get. There was no bargain here that I could see, just distress and loss on both sides. [Bennett, 2005, p. 34]

Thank you, Alan, for your untold story. It was the distress and loss on all sides for my son, my daughter, his father, and myself that would drive me on.

At the same time I have to acknowledge that the concept of the schizophregenic (schizophrenia inducing) mother and family does exist. I only have two examples in my direct experience, but I feel it is important to record them.

Example 1

> I was working as a sessional psychotherapist in a private mental health hospital. A couple came to see me, mistakenly thinking that I knew their daughter's overall treatment plan. Their daughter was currently on one of the wards. She had bipolar disorder and suffered from psychotic episodes. It was perhaps her sixth time in hospital. Her mother described her stay in hospital over the Christmas period as being very inconvenient for the family. The mother did most of the talking. She told me her daughter nearly died from an infection when she was fourteen. It was after this near death experience that she became psychotic. Since then she had tried to commit suicide several times. Because parental guilt is a normal response to suicide attempts and near death experiences, I asked them together how they were coping with any feelings of guilt. The mother snapped, "I have nothing to feel guilty about." The father replied, "I feel guilty all the time." The mother admonished him immediately. "That is because you have always had a soft spot for her. You are being ridiculous when she has been nothing but trouble."

Example 2

> Dimitri was not a patient of mine. His story came to my attention in another context. He told me of his first marriage, a long time ago now, to an Irish Roman Catholic woman who suffered from manic depression. They had two sons. After the first few years of marriage, she was categorically determined to bring them up as a one-parent family. She was overtly hostile and as difficult as possible towards him and the children. He left, but tried to be a good father and take them out to football. The eldest son refused to see his father from the age of eight on the instructions of his mother. The mother kept the boys locked in their rooms in the evening and they weren't allowed into the living room. She treated them like animals. When they were young adolescents and started to go out, if they were later than 10 p.m. the door would be locked and they would have to sleep rough. Both boys developed psychosis. The eldest boy has been in and out of institutions all his life. The younger son, who is doing well on medication, is now living with his girlfriend and has recently started working. He has developed a good relationship with his father, and he is an excellent example of the medical model working well.

> Dimitri had another two sons with his second wife. He has a good relationship with them and they suffer from no mental illnesses.

The recognition of the existence of the schizophregenic mother led on to the development of a more complex causal theory, often referred to as "the communications within families theory". This hypothesis, which goes beyond previous theories, which focused on the neurological pathways of the brain or psychological breakdown of the ego, explores the family atmosphere and looks at such issues as over-protectiveness or excessive control.

However, as Franz Ruppert (2002) points out, "It is not made clear what causes the parents' behaviour, why a psychosis-inducing atmosphere is created, and where such confusing communication within the family comes from" (p. 16) and why some individuals respond by becoming psychotic and others do not.

Laing's work, while undoubtedly valuable in its capacity to radically challenge the traditional views and treatments of psychosis, also stops short of addressing the issue of unpredictable patterns of psychosis within the same family.

The truth is, people with psychosis come from a wide variety of family backgrounds and social influences. Cannabis-induced psychosis has introduced a new genre of possible causal influences into the melting pot, drawing in different types of family from a wide range of cultural and ethnic backgrounds. Is it not time to begin considering that maybe there is something of value in all the theories?

CHAPTER FOUR

Finding kindred spirits

Diary extract

I look straight ahead of me into the pale blue eyes of my therapist. Her silver, bobbed hair framed her face, her eyes were focused directly on me. It hurt when I looked at her. She was mirroring back to me my sadness and despair. When I saw it like this, it felt too much to bear. I knew she heard me. I knew she empathized with me. She was a great therapist and a wise woman I had come to trust and admire. My despair hung in the therapy room like a wispy, silver-grey mantle, but when I left it followed me home. It was mine and mine alone. I wished I could leave it with my therapist. I wished I could leave it anywhere.

My weekly therapy was a source of great comfort to me. Here, in the therapy room, with its faded curtains and antique furniture, I could be myself with all my worries and neuroses. I looked forward to going, to escape from the daily toil of my mortal coil. It was a time to reflect; a time to have my neurotic beliefs challenged; a time to relate as the real me, the broken me, the disillusioned me.

But I was not always broken; sometimes I had issues. Again and again I brought my concerns about my son's therapist. How I wished I had never instigated the process, how I did not know what was going on, how I imagined I had reasons not to trust him. How I did not want to stop my son's therapy. How I felt trapped by the situation, and on and on I went.

Not only that but I was also still under pressure from my ex. I had not yet realized that psychosis in the family played havoc with relationships. Men and women traditionally and habitually respond to crises differently in any event. The psychotic tentacles of confused thought and feeling helpless left no one untouched. There were no cosy visits to the hospital with grapes and magazines; all the things that make the family feel better. No treatment plan that could be discussed with the patient; just round and roundabout discussions that led nowhere.

My ex could not understand why I was pursuing all these alternative therapies. He had never heard of them. Why wasn't I doing something more? Why could I not get proper treatment? I did not only hear what my ex said; I imagined things, too. I imagined he thought I was stupid, and a new age nut. I heard only personal criticism and complaints about me and my actions. And then I did what I have always done. I didn't reply. I didn't take my own position. I just closed down. It was as if an invisible elastoplast had been placed over my mouth; the invisible plaster that has been with me since my childhood. I did not know how to reply without screaming and yelling, and so I said nothing. I didn't communicate. I punished him and left him with nowhere to go until he ran out of steam and had no real idea what had been going on.

My therapist put her head slowly to one side. She gently reflected back to me that maybe I had issues of fear with males in authority. She reminded me that my son's therapist and my ex were both trying to help in their own ways. She wondered how I felt about this. How did I feel about males in authority? I was stunned. I had never considered this before. My defence mechanisms leapt into place. It was not true. I had good relationships with men in authority. I pointed this out to her much too quickly, in crisp tones. It was just the therapist and my ex who were presently being unreasonable. They should know how I felt without me telling them.

Oh, oh, oh, all my issues were coming up for review. I wanted to play the victim. I wanted to feel right and for people to feel compassion for my plight. Surely this was not the time to look fair and square at my own illogical and sometimes insane responses.

But I listened to my therapist. She asked me to go home and write a letter of forgiveness and gratitude to my ex that I would never send. In the letter I told him how grateful I was for his part in providing support during our son's illness and how much I appreciated his direct male approach. How I regretted I could not communicate with him better. How I heard his very real concern, and finally I thanked him for being the father of our son.

I realize in writing this that it sounds as if I wrote that letter willingly and with good grace. Nothing could be further from the truth. From the vantage point of the present, I can see and appreciate all that my ex-husband did, but back then I was blinded by my own self-importance. I felt it was all down to *me* (oh oh oh, here I go again), *my* misperceptions, *my* tunnel vision, *my* habitual way of thinking and relating to the world. Writing the letter was the first tentative step to ending the internal and external blame-game and the beginning of some sort of personal responsibility, to act consciously and with an awareness of choice. I had, as the phrase goes in therapy, been "acting out". I was hurt and defended and had been acting out all my unconscious responses to dealing with the crisis that came in the wake of the illness. All the things I had learnt to do as a child floated to the surface. Closing down and feeling a victim was my habitual way of being; the one that I had learnt as a child under the fierce interrogation of my depressed mother.

I could not believe that all this was coming up now. But there was more. My wise, wonderful, silver-haired therapist, with shed-loads of compassion and empathy, did not fill the empty hole in me. I had to admit she was the best therapist I had had. Before that, I had two real shockers. Being a transpersonal psychotherapist is no guarantee of being a good one. Just as in any profession, there are outstanding ones, mediocre ones, and truly average ones. I was lucky enough to have an outstanding therapist; she certainly was not letting me languish in victimhood, but something was missing. I knew she had not shared my experience. How could she know how I felt when confronted with the crazy reality of psychosis, with all its terror and incomprehensibility no longer subordinated to the supreme control of my son's complete personality? How could she feel the agonizing split in me between totally loving my son and

hating the psychosis? I began to feel a deep need to talk to someone who had shared my experiences and all the deeply conflicting
emotions that went with them. How could she know how let down
and thwarted I felt by psychiatry and its lack of coherent theories?

I was in my final year of college by now. I had been on track to
do an MA relating to what I thought were the huge challenges of
being fifty-plus. So, my chosen topic had been "In what way does
being 50+ enhance the emergence of the authentic self?" I was
going to follow the work of Carl Jung, who has been called the
"father of second half of life psychology". Whereas Freud focused
on the childhood stages of development, Jung focused on what is
sometimes called second adulthood, and the opportunities for integrating the conscious and the unconscious into the "self". The "self"
symbolized the totality of the self, through accessing all the unconscious, repressed, and denied parts of ourselves. As I had already
trained as a Life Coach and worked as an Executive Coach, I had
ideas of lucratively capitalizing on working with the fifty-plus age
bracket in the corporate market, which would command a very
different salary to that of a psychotherapist.

But, by this time, what age I was, my fear of fading, my cellulite,
and how much I couldn't earn did not seem of the slightest relevance. I was finding my real self all right, through my unconscious
responses to the crisis and adversity of living with psychosis. The
extremes of the situation were bringing out the extremes of reaction
within me. I felt as if I was imprisoned and trapped by psychosis,
yet I felt I needed to address it. I decided to work with phenome-
nology. The phenomenon of what was presenting itself in my life
right now, and that phenomenon was loving someone in psychosis.

I decided I could not commit to an MA, and opted instead to
qualify for a Diploma in Transpersonal Psychotherapy through the
organization, facilitation, and documentation of a workshop,
which, together with my case studies and essays, would earn me
my psychotherapy accreditation. I decided to run a workshop for
other people, just like me, who were struggling to find their way
through the thicket of psychosis, its treatments, and lack of them.
At the time I was not yet fully aware of the stigma attached to the
word "schizophrenia", so I decided to call my workshop "Does
Someone You Love Have Schizophrenia?" I took the idea to my
group supervisor. I remember seeing her eyes widen when I named

my project and remember her commenting that it would be very challenging. We had several weekends of group supervision to prepare us for our final projects. I felt extremely anxious about mine, as I had no previous experience of attending, never mind running, such a workshop.

And so I set about writing my Project Proposal from a transpersonal perspective, which, while acknowledging the importance of individual experience, adopts a wide perspective in its awareness of our interconnectedness and the mystery of life with all its unanswerable questions.

Project proposal

Part one: inspiration

"And the Puzzle in Therapy is not how did I get this way, but what does my angel want with me?" (Hillman & Ventura, 1993, p. 70).

My Current Belief System: I do not want my son to believe his own thoughts. I want it to be different. It should not be happening to him or me. I want to change the situation. However, what I am saying is that I want to change reality. My thoughts are arguing with reality. I can only see what my ego wants me to see. The only time we suffer is when we believe a thought that argues with what is. What is, is. I have to remember that this is one small part in the soul's journey. I therefore write my hypothesis from the viewpoint of what is the purpose of what is happening in my life? What does my angel want with me?

Part two: hypothesis

My hypothesis is that caring for a loved one with schizophrenia provides transformational opportunities for emotional, mental, and spiritual growth. (Definition of carer: someone who temporarily has more for those who temporarily have less.)

My own experience has been that the onset of schizophrenia introduces a transformational crisis not only into the patient's life, but also into the whole family unit. All are plunged from operating in a world of consensus reality into dealing on a daily basis with altered and extreme states of consciousness. That which is normally repressed into the unconscious or forms part of a dreaming world becomes everyday conversation. The carers are forced to make changes in the way they relate to someone outside of consensus reality, and are confronted with the limitations of their firmly established belief systems as to what constitutes consciousness and everyday reality.

Part three: proposal

To offer a support group over a weekend, so that these experiences can be shared. I would like to own at this early stage that the purpose of forming a group would be as much for my benefit as the participants. One of my beliefs is that we give what we want to receive, and this is my gift to those travelling a similar path to my own. Although I would facilitate it as a professional, I have no answers, only more questions.

I added some notes: that I was in a very dark place and that my faith was being severely tested. The honest truth was that if I did have an angel, I felt it was doing a pretty lousy job. I knew the theory, but it was difficult to walk my talk. Anyway, it kept me busy and I was doing something for me that might help others. I felt I had no other option, because no other topic interested me.

Meanwhile back at home, we had now moved house. It kept me occupied, but even that could not fully divert my attention. My daughter and her boyfriend had returned. But there seemed little to celebrate; they had not really want to curtail their travelling, and I had forgotten what enjoying myself was. I was subsumed in the misery of the illness and did not know how to shake it off. Siblings of psychotic patients often get a rotten deal, and my daughter was no exception. But it did help to be able to share some experiences. I still didn't know what to say about my son to my friends or my fellow students. My daughter summed it up by saying that if someone asked her how he was, she wished they hadn't, as she didn't know what to say. But, on the other hand, if they didn't ask, she considered them heartless and rude. It really was a no-win situation.

Our new house brought new experiences. It was in the heart of Islington, in a quiet street, near lots of restaurants with tables out on the street. As I walked back from the supermarket past the welcoming cafés, I could not help but notice the candlelit tables, the ubiquitous wine glasses, and the animated faces. I felt these people belonged to a different universe, one I no longer was part of. I felt bitter, I, too, longed to be carefree and having fun, but that bloody grey mantle followed me everywhere.

Christmas came and went. My son had some days absolutely free of symptoms. We crossed our fingers and hoped for a reprieve from the Gods. But a film on television seemed to send him back to whence he had come. A New Year, but I had no heart to make any resolutions. My workshop was quite soon. How I, of all people, could run it I had no idea. I didn't know how to hope any more.

Our situation remained the same but not quite. One day my son came home from therapy and announced he had told his therapist to "F off". He said categorically that he was not going back. I know this formed part of his symptoms and the illness. A little bit of me even felt sorry for the therapist. But it was a small bit. I breathed a temporary sigh of relief. I had one less issue to worry about but it was like taking a straw off the camel's back.

Then it was Mother's Day. My son gave me a book entitled *When Bad Things Happen to Good People* (Kushner, 1981). My son might be ill, but he was not mad; his heart and soul were intact. I read the book in a day. It somehow helped when I read

> Are you capable of forgiving and accepting in love a world which has disappointed you by not being perfect, a world in which there is so much unfairness and cruelty, disease and crime, earthquake and accident? Can you forgive its imperfections and love it because it is capable of containing great beauty and goodness, and because it is the only world we have? [*ibid.*, p. 174]

I had to keep on believing.

Reflections on finding kindred spirits

One of my main motivations for running the workshop came from my deep disappointment at reading some of the available books and pamphlets on how to care for someone with psychosis. Of course, the books contained a great deal of essential, practical, and useful information. In particular, *Understanding and Helping the Schizophrenic: A Guide for Family and Friends* (Arieti, 1981) shows a profound understanding and respect for both the illness and the family and I can heartily recommend it, although the depersonalizing use of the word "schizophrenic" indicates the times in which it was written. I also recommend E. Fuller Torrey's (2006) *Surviving Schizophrenia: A Manual for Families, Patients and Providers*. It is written by him as both a clinical and research psychiatrist but in acknowledgement of his sister's diagnosis of schizophrenia. It is an indispensable guide and its purpose is to enhance awareness of the progress of schizophrenia and the possible ways in which it may develop. However, it was the very reasonableness of most of the texts in describing the emotional fall-out on the family that left me both inflamed and wanting.

> Living with a patient day by day becomes a therapeutic task, and, indeed, not an easy one even for the most cooperative family. [Arieti, 1981, p. 138]

> When any group of people live together or spend significant time together, conflicts are inevitable. No one agrees all the time! When one family member has schizophrenia, conflict in the household is even more likely because of the symptoms of the illness. [Mueser & Gingerich, 1994, p. 128]

> Developing the right attitude is the single most important thing an individual or family can do to survive schizophrenia. [Torrey, 2006, p. 318).

Basically, the message is, "It is not easy, conflict is likely and developing the right attitude is important." Gggggrrrr. What right attitude? I most certainly have attitude. I have an attitude problem to psychosis. It drives me crazy. It makes me climb up the walls with frustration and anger. It makes me throw my hairbrush across the room and shake my fist at God.

No, it is not easy, I want to scream at the books. It is one of the most difficult psychological challenges that humans ever face; trying to reach out to someone you love who adamantly believes in another reality. How can we learn to deal with this? Professional mental health carers might have to talk to people in psychotic states five days a week, nine to five, but they do not have the emotional involvement of love. They can go home at the end of the day to their sane homes. As Phaedrus, the main character in *Zen and the Art of Motorcyle Maintenance*, says, "... they're not *kin* ... not of a *kind* ... same root ... *kind*ness ... they can't have real *kind*ness toward him, they're not his *kin*" (Pirsig, 1999, p. 67). Their hearts don't break. They often do not know the personality who was there before; that coherent person, with consistent patterns of behaviour that you knew and loved, and who was once well. How can they know what patterns of behaviour are normal for someone they never knew in the first place?

This is what I could not find in some of these well-intentioned and valuable books. At worst, they were books of reason, about living with unreason, by experts with no personal experience of loving someone in an altered state of consciousness. There was no real recognition or empathy for the deep well of long-term emotional despair psychosis invokes in every family member. They were great at conveying practical information, but not one of them addressed the extremely complex emotional roller-coaster that came from loving someone and sometimes loathing their psychotic behaviour, and the ensuing feelings of rage, frustration, helplessness, hopelessness, despair, guilt, shame, and isolation. These were the issues I wanted to address in the weekend.

Having thought that I had abandoned Carl Jung when I gave up my MA, it was to Jung I now turned for inspiration. Jung had gained his knowledge of the unconscious from nine years of working as a psychiatrist with psychotic patients. In 1909, he had been invited to America to "receive an honorary degree, largely for his work on schizophrenia—his principal area of expert knowledge" (Tallis, 2002, p. 87). At the risk of being repetitive, I would like to iterate that no other illness invites us to delve so deeply into how the mind works. It was Jung's work with psychotic patients that helped lead him to formalize his theories of the unconscious, which went way beyond what Freud had discovered.

But it was not Jung's extensive theories of the unconscious that drew my attention at this stage, but his description of the dissociations in psychosis that produce the personalities that appear in delusions and hallucinations.

The split-off figures assume banal, grotesque, or highly exagger-
ated names and characters, and are often objectionable in many
other ways. They do not, moreover, co-operate with the patient's
consciousness. They are not tactful and they have no respect for
sentimental values. On the contrary they break in and make a
disturbance at any time, they torment the ego in a hundred ways;
all are objectionable and shocking either in their noisy and imper-
tinent behaviour or in their grotesque cruelty and obscenity. [De
Laszlo, 1990, pp. 97–98]

This empathetic recognition of the unwelcome and bullying
aspects of psychosis in the family inspired me to try to create a safe
and supportive weekend group where these potentially shame-
inducing experiences could be shared. All I had to go on was how
I was being affected and how isolating it felt. I just had to trust that
I was not alone in my experiences.

Even before the workshop, I received calls from people asking
to meet with me. One lady came to see me in despair about her
daughter who, although on medication, was still acting strangely.
The daughter was white-skinned, but believed she was black. She
wore an Afro wig and make-up to darken her skin. Bizarrely, she
only went out in the early hours of the morning. The mother, who
had a full time job, followed her as she roamed the streets in an
attempt to protect her. She was exhausted from these nocturnal
excursions. But one of the most revealing aspects of this hour-long
session was that I could not get the mother to talk about anything
but her daughter. Time and again, I would ask how the situation
made her feel, but she had no interest in herself; she was lost in her
daughter's nightmare journey.

I realized this was going to be a big issue at the weekend. How
was I going to get the participants to talk about their personal feelings and interactions with their loved ones rather than getting
totally lost in the stories? It would be absolutely no use giving them
quotes like "One must know oneself in order to understand others"
(Dorman, 2003, p. 126). I would just have to wait and see how they
would respond.

I decided to hold the workshop at my college and, on the advice
of my supervisor, limited the number to just six, so that everyone
would have enough time to tell their story. All the participants were
women, four mothers and two sisters.

And so the Saturday of the workshop dawned at last. I arrived at college in plenty of time only to discover that they had all turned up early and were down in the far from glamorous basement kitchen making tea. When I somewhat nervously went to collect them, I could not believe my eyes. They were chattering away as if they had known each other all their lives. The workshop had started and I wasn't even there.

One of my major concerns was the thorny, and much debated issue, of self-disclosure on the part of the facilitator. I had spent hours thinking about this. What if they knew how broken I felt? Would they all head straight for the door? They were all aware that I had personal experience because I had already told them when they applied. However, my fears proved to be ill founded. Within the first minute of sitting down in the group therapy room, before any introductions, one of the mothers said to me, "You have a son who is ill, haven't you?" As I nodded in assent, she said, "I wouldn't have come if you hadn't." The rest of the group nodded in agreement. And that was that. They had come to talk about themselves and their loved ones and didn't need or want any personal input from me.

And so we moved on to the introductions and what had brought them to the workshop. It is generally acknowledged that group work starts long before the participants gather together. The sense that they had found a safe place in which to share their stories must have been building up in each and every one of them for days or even weeks. However, I had not expected that within five minutes four of the participants would be in tears. I had not quite registered the possibility of this immediate intensity of feeling.

And so their narratives unfolded. Shattered lives, broken dreams, and rivers of tears flowed. Not one of them alluded to their own selves or feelings. Their stories were all about their loved ones.

> *Maria*: Her son had taken drugs at university. Later, he came home to live with her, but when he became violent she threw him out. He had gone to live in a bedsit until he was hospitalized. She was consumed with guilt that she had not realized how ill he was. He was now living on his own and was on medication and state benefit. Because of the side-effects of the drugs, he was six stone overweight and deeply depressed. Maria lived in a constant state of anxiety as he hated the medication and regularly came off it.

Celia: Her daughter had become addicted to drugs at university and had attempted suicide. When hospitalized she was diagnosed with schizophrenia. Seven years later, her daughter was still on medication, living at home, and socially isolated except for meetings of Narcotics Anonymous. She was five stone overweight from the side-effects of the drugs, and very depressed about this.

Francine: Her son had been ill for thirteen years. He was on medication, and massively overweight. His condition of schizophrenia was compounded by diabetes. She said he behaved as if he was three years old, constantly asking for affection.

Colleen: Her son had suffered from schizophrenia for nearly twenty years. He was now living in an assisted flat nearby. She had looked after him for fifteen years. She felt the worst was over and she didn't want to talk about it. He was on medication, but had no life and no friends. The weekend workshop had been a gift from a friend.

Amy: Her younger brother was on medication for schizophrenia and lived with a sympathetic friend nearby. She sensed she was his only link with the world and felt she had to look out for him. She tried to shield her elderly parents from the horrors of it all. The previous weekend he had taken heavy-duty drugs, and she was furious with him. She felt he had an irresponsible attitude to his illness. She had no one to talk to.

Yvette: Her elder sister had suffered from schizophrenia for fifteen years. Her illness was marked by violent and aggressive behaviour towards the family. She worried constantly about what would happen when her parents died.

In listening to them, I was especially conscious that the weekend was a problem-focused support group that was not designed either to confront or open up issues beyond what was presented. Psychosis in the family was enough to deal with. My intention was to let the group unfold in its own way and in its own time, with the classic humanistic ingredients of support, empathy, and unconditional positive regard. Once trust was established, we could begin to do some experiential exercises. And so I began by asking them what they most wanted from the weekend and what they most feared. Once the tears had stopped, they were keen to participate.

They all shared the expectation that they would be able to tell their stories and hear the stories of others. They wanted to rekindle hope together and learn some additional coping strategies. They wanted to know how to act effectively from a place of self-preservation and avoid feeling ridiculed. On the other hand, they were afraid that they would have too many emotional outbursts and go home more depressed. Paradoxically, they were worried that they would be advised to detach even more, and confront objectively the hard fact that schizophrenia meant a life-long sentence of medication that offered no real hope.

Intuitively, following the feeling of the group, I suggested we start the workshop with a short ritual. A ritual is a way of impressing the unconscious in a conscious way. I had taken along a small selection of stones and I invited them each to choose one to represent their loved one. They took a great deal of time over this, making sure that they felt they had the "right one". They were then invited to hold the stone and to say a silent prayer for the highest good of their relative. We then replaced the stones in the centre of the room, where they remained throughout the weekend. There are no words for these experiences. Their solemn, pained faces were testament enough. I was doing what I most wanted to do for my son, simple prayer. Each time we left the room and came back in, we would reaffirm our silent prayers for them. Through a crisis, we realize how little we control our lives. This is a way of letting go of the idea that all is hopeless and requires no particular system of belief.

And it wasn't all about tears. Amazingly, in the safety of shared experience, there was even laughter without a hint of ridicule. Maria introduced this humour early on the opening morning when she told us about the time her son, on being discharged from hospital, had been assigned a one-bedroomed flat in a large, high-rise block designated for those with mental health problems. She said that it didn't seem to her to be the best plan to have him live with a load of other "nutters". Everyone in the room laughed. When I drew their attention to it, they said it was such an overwhelming relief to be able to talk about it in the complete safety of shared understanding. It had been everyone's experience that they guarded their language to almost everybody about the horrors of their situations.

But my greatest challenge was not getting them to talk, but getting them to talk about themselves, their own feelings and responses. They were somehow all lost in their loved one's experiences. Just as their loved ones were lost in psychosis, so were they. To counteract this, I invited them to tell stories about themselves, their hopes, aspirations, values, and dreams. This was a turning point. Suddenly the energy changed from burdened care-givers to six very alive, talented women. They were actively supporting each other and noticing for the first time the numerous talents, courage, and wealth of experience in the room. I realized that I was in the presence of warm, sane, intelligent, loving people desperately trying to help their loved ones.

Supporting each other in the acknowledgement of their strength and resilience undoubtedly helped each member of the group to identify and develop more effective methods of dealing with some of their problems. Maria, who emerged as the spokesperson in the group, said she had initially felt critical of my suggestion that she talk about herself rather than her son but afterwards realized how liberating it had been.

As guilt featured as a major player in all of their stories I gave them a small handout I had adapted from *Cognitive Behaviour Therapy* (Neenan & Dryden, 2002).

Guilt

Guilt often involves people assuming too much responsibility for the people they love and the events that happen to them. This excessive sense of responsibility comes from the "omni" outlook. Tackling the "omni outlook" starts with reminding ourselves of our status as a fallible being, not an all-powerful deity. Because people cannot possibly meet these God-like standards of behaviour, they feel guilty and "less than". The facts of the circumstances that have happened need reviewing and a new acceptance of our limited knowledge (omniscience), control of others (omnipotence), ability to be in the right place at the right time (omnipresence), and our limited levels of competence (omnicompetence) need acknowledging.

Omniscience

"I should have known my son was schizophrenic and not just violent."

This assumes that she should have known about the presenting symptoms when, in fact, her knowledge of them was non-existent at the time. This is an assumption that she should know everything, as would a deity.

Omnipotence

"I should have been able to help stop my daughter taking drugs."

This is an assumption of God-like powers. We can only be held accountable for our own behaviour. To believe otherwise is a form of omnipotent thinking.

Omnipresent

"I should have been there to stop her."

We can only be in one place at a time. Only God is everywhere. Human beings are often in the wrong place at the wrong time, and this is an example of omnipresent thinking.

Omnicompetent

"I should have been able to deal with the drug taking better."

This is an attempt to be totally effectively in any given situation. Expertise is not guaranteed, nor is success necessarily achievable, so this is an example of omnicompetent thinking.

Sharing their stories of human fallibility, and hearing feedback that they could have done no more, enabled all the participants to develop more realistic expectations of what they could or could not achieve or, indeed, have power over.

We discovered how our unconscious coping mechanisms were worn to a frazzle. Everyone felt that they did not really cope, but just managed to survive. As we explored further, we realized that we all had different coping mechanisms. We all kept on doing what we had always done in difficult times, only we did it even more. As we talked, the differences in our learnt ways of being in the world came to the fore.

Maria tried to minimize the impact on her life by rearranging her already tight timetables, as her son took up all the extra time. Making timetables made her feel in some sort of control. She tried to maintain as much normality as possible, but with great strain to herself.

Celia concentrated on everyone else's feelings in the family. She didn't know how any of them coped, from the grandparents to the siblings to aunts and uncles. She tried to take care of all the family members and then felt angry when no one paid any attention to her. She knew it was a no-win situation, but was terrified to look at her own pain in case she collapsed.

Francine coped through extended maternal mode and selfless martyrdom. She took no time at all for herself and shouldered all the responsibility while, at the same time, feeling resentful. She said her husband took no responsibility and she felt she had two patients to look after. Some days she felt like running away.

Colleen pretended it wasn't happening and that it no longer hurt.

Amy believed it was all her responsibility and she couldn't let go for a moment. She believed she had to shield her parents. She wished she could feel less responsible.

Yvette concentrated on choosing to believe in the perfection of life itself. She would not acknowledge that she was in any pain.

Again and again, throughout the group process, I used my own experiences to help me assess what might be needed. Our discussions led me to recall a time when I blamed everyone for not wanting to listen to my problems. Fortunately, with some therapeutic help, I had come to realize that the downside of blaming others is that we become unable to assume the kind of personal responsibility that would enable us to initiate useful changes. Recognizing an element of this dynamic, I asked them to write down three examples of blaming others, using a form adapted from *Cognitive Behaviour Therapy* (Neenan & Dryden, 2002), which they then read to each other. To illustrate the process, I include the example "Taking control", shown at the top of the next page.

Through sharing their experiences in this way, they were surprised to discover how much they all blamed their loved ones

Taking control. Blaming others for your problems will result in not being able to take responsibility for the changes you would like to make. Think of recent problems where you blamed, then rewrite the problem so you take control of it.

Blaming others	Taking control
No one wants to listen to my real problems.	I now choose to tell my deepest fears to my therapist.

for the way they acted without fully appreciating how much psychosis dictated their behavioural responses. They also realized how much they blamed other family members for failing to provide sympathetic understanding.

However, it was the finding of kindred spirits that was the most appreciated aspect of the weekend. A sense of kinship helped to decrease feelings of shame, inadequacy, and isolation as we came to realize that we are neither unique nor alone in our pain and suffering. By acknowledging that we were sometimes weak, and sometimes strong and courageous, we were able to reinforce each other's positive self image.

As the weekend drew to a close, a common theme emerged of having watched our loved ones experience a living hell. A living hell marked by incomprehensible behaviour patterns and a withdrawal into a reality that we could not enter. What we unanimously agreed was that when our loved ones entered their living hell, we entered with them.

Everyone acknowledged the immediate cohesive quality that had manifested the moment the group came together, and they suggested we form an ongoing support group. This support group met many times over the years, and has been yet another inspiration for this book.

However, Colleen, who received the workshop as a gift from a friend, did not form part of the ongoing support group. She was in a different place, where she wanted to start to live her life again despite her son's long-term, disabling illness. She said she had given up fifteen years of her life and it was time to move on. This theme recurs again and again in long-term cases. Even though we might all love someone in psychosis, we are not always on the same part of the journey. Groups that deal with the need to accept and move on are to be encouraged as well. It is a deeply painful experience to have to get on with life and let someone you love remain isolated and withdrawn.

With the workshop over it was time for me to write up the experience and reflect on my findings. This is part of what I wrote.

> The long-term nature of psychosis leads to burn-out and a desire to find more effective coping strategies.
>
> We all experienced and mirrored some unconscious behaviour patterns associated with psychosis; e.g. isolation, social contraction, high levels of anxiety, paranoia and loss of sense of self.
>
> A common theme was the experience of a "living hell".
>
> Everyone expressed a sense of hopelessness associated with conventional psychiatric approaches.
>
> We had all become aware of our ability to love the unlovable and acknowledged the constant source of love within our hearts.
>
> We all expressed a desire to believe in a Higher Power.

Running the workshop highlighted the fact that my own "coping mechanisms" were mine and mine alone. When I heard Maria talking about keeping everything as "normal" as possible, I realized how I had withdrawn into my "only child" place. I had felt that nobody could or would understand what I was going through. With an absent father and a narcissistic mother, this was my prevailing belief.

On a transpersonal level, I began to suspect that I have aspects to my nature that make me different from my family and my culture. I came to realize that, in witnessing the suffering of psychosis, I had to acknowledge the diabolical forces that exist in the unconscious. I unwillingly had to admit that there is an order in the universe that includes darkness, disease, and the unknown. Yet, it was in these unknown dark places that I discovered strengths I never knew that went beyond the feelings of aloneness of the only child. The most salient piece of learning that the group shared was that whatever the loved one in psychosis did, however crazy or deluded or abusive, we went on loving them. Even though I had coped inadequately and felt lost and hurt, there remained, somehow, within me a constant source of renewal of love within my heart. I began to glimpse the tragedy behind identifying with my idea of myself as simply an individual ego and seeing myself as separate from everyone and everything.

I drew comfort from the quote "There is no human response that I experience today that someone else will not experience tomorrow or has not already done" (The Teresian Carmelites, 2004, p. 41). That somehow seemed to ease my wounding, if only briefly.

Afternote to workshop

When I reflected on my workshop, I did not have the insight to realize that my group consisted only of mothers and sisters, e.g., parents and siblings. So, as a representation of psychosis in the family, it did not include the huge and often devastating psychological impact on children with parents with psychosis.

However, both my case studies were of men whose lives had also been shaped by psychosis. So I include them now. The case studies were written from several different approaches (integrative) and included the family history and the story of the therapy. It is only now that I have any real understanding of the psychological trauma that children undergo when one of their parents is psychotic. However, the psychological trauma of psychosis in the family is felt by every member and leaves no one untouched. This fact needs now to be acknowledged in psychotherapy.

Case study

John came to therapy (aged forty) initially because he always found himself in abusive and dysfunctional relationships.

His family history included his mother being diagnosed with schizophrenia when he was five. His whole life and personality had been shaped by his mother's psychotic episodes, with his weekends often spent visiting her in various institutions over many years. Again and again he would tell me that, as an adolescent, he fantasized about matricide. His relationship with his mother was normal in one respect. He loved her and he hated the psychosis. At one point, in his teens, he made a vow never to laugh again. Even though his parents were both highly educated and he was extremely intelligent, he had never pursued any formal higher education. He recognized his inner rebellion against conforming to any of society's expectations.

Psychosis in the family often propels family members into therapy, where they seek a stable relationship and positive mirroring. Both John's brother and sister were also in therapy. John was in therapy for five years. During that time he gained a degree and an MA, and left therapy shortly before his impending marriage.

Case study

> Robert entered therapy (aged fifty) because of depression. He had a two-day-a-week job and was in a long-term partnership with Alice. She suffered from severe depression and had never been able to work. Her mother had suffered from psychotic episodes while Alice was growing up. She was unable to take any responsibility for her own life, and consistently undermined and criticized Robert and blamed him for her depression. Her behaviour was unpredictable, and often aggressive. He knew, however, that he would never leave her because he realized she was unable to live on her own.

In my case study, I again failed spectacularly at naming the psychological traumatic impact of psychosis on even the extended family. Alice's depression was intrinsically linked to her relationship with her often hospitalized mother. It was hard for Robert to come to terms with maybe Alice never being well, even with a medley of medications. He came to understand her utter dependence on him, and felt considerable relief on realizing that he was not the root cause of her depression.

Robert left therapy when his career was thriving and he was on the verge of having his first novel published.

CHAPTER FIVE

Surrendering

Diary extract

The most terrible thing has happened. It is so terrible I do not recognize it. I have done what all human beings do. I have adapted to our circumstances. I have not adjusted well, become accepting, or surrendered, but I have begun to outwardly normalize external events to compensate for my inner chaos. Our unwelcome guest has become a regular feature of our lives. It never ceases to shock me, or send my solar plexus into another orbit, but the incipient fear has become a routine part of life.

A long time ago, I swore this would never happen to me. I remember my beloved, darling Nana dying slowly of bone cancer. She would whisper to me, "I feel as if every bone in my body is rotting." She had no idea of her diagnosis or prognosis. I did not know what to say, so I would wait a while and pat her hand and ask her if she wanted chocolate ice-cream. My mother nursed her at home. I remember going round for my early evening visit and my mother telling me elatedly that she had eaten a quarter of a sandwich for tea. The unspoken hope was that maybe she would eat more tomorrow and recover from being a six-stone skeleton. I knew it was crazy then. I knew that we had all lost the plot. I knew that we clung to whatever piece of normality we could. The quarter of a sandwich for tea meant that soon she would not eat anything and would soon die. I knew this when I did not even know how the human mind works. I knew normality was whatever we pretended it to be.

And there I was again, completely sucked into my automatic responses of normalizing things without any conscious awareness of my survival strategies. I may have run a workshop and rigorously observed our coping mechanisms, but I was human and my unconscious defence mechanisms were protecting me and meant I did not feel the incredible pain I was in. My hurting heart was bypassed as I busied myself with keeping going and trying to think things through. I lived in constant fear, but by then that was normal. I hardly went out except to work and that was normal too. I was hyper-vigilant and that was normal too.

My son now had a new process orientated therapist recommended by my therapist. Process work, which first appeared on the scene in the 1970s, is a therapeutic approach developed by the Jungian analyst, Arnold Mindell. Mindell began researching illness as a meaningful expression of the unconscious mind, and *City Shadows* (1990) explores psychological interventions in psychiatry. This is an approach that views psychotic states as momentary or evolving cyclical processes that have an implicit order, purpose, and direction. It gave me hope.

Before starting the therapy with my son, the therapist invited me to meet him. He listened attentively, applauded my approach, and felt for my pain. I had the greatest difficulty restraining an impulse to kiss him when I left, so relieved was I to be treated with dignity. My son now went regularly to see him. It was a great relief, but all the energy I had expended on worrying about the other therapist had just given me something on which to project my unhappiness. My unhappiness was now deeply rooted and embedded in my way of being. We were surviving and things were not deteriorating and my son had an experienced therapist whom I felt I could trust.

On the orthomolecular nutritional front, the gaps of six weeks between the treatments at the Brain Bio Centre seemed too long. Although they offered expert professional nutritional support programmes, there was no psychiatric or psychotherapeutic back up. I somehow felt that we needed more.

From my Internet searches I discovered that Canada, home of the International Schizophrenia Foundation (ISF), leads the world in orthomolecular treatment for psychosis. The ISF, with its world-wide network of affiliates, promotes orthomolecular treatment to enable people with schizophrenia, and other mental illness, to lead healthy, independent lives. For thirty-eight years they have been holding annual international conferences focusing on nutritional medicine for mental illnesses, with a particular emphasis on psychosis. From my little laptop in Islington, I sat and puzzled over how it could possibly be that the forty-year-old ISF was so little evident in Britain.

As ever, with my desperation-driven busy boots on, I wrote to them requesting a list of orthomolecular psychiatrists in London. Their response revealed that their numbers equaled zero. This was four years ago. But they sent me a list of English subscribers to their quarterly newsletter, and I wrote to all six of them.

Is Canada really that far from England? I felt as if it might as well be on another planet. I tried in vain to talk to people about orthomolecular psychiatry, but blank faces and blank minds were all I got in response. Times have moved on, however, and there is now widespread recognition that the food we eat affects mental health and behaviour. The Mental Health Foundation produced an influential report *Feeding Minds* (2006), and there is growing aware-ness of the possible importance of omega-3 essential fatty acids for healthy brain function.

My letters to the UK ISF subscription list produced several replies, including one from the doctor who founded the British Society of Integrated Medicine (BSIM). The BSIM is a professional membership organization that leads the UK field in championing the principles, practice, and development of integrated medicine. This approach promotes the safest and most effective approaches and treatments from the world of conventional and complementary medicine. Hurrah, but at the time they did not have a psychiatric division. None the less, I had a medical practitioner to turn to, as this doctor also ran a clinic.

Hoping against hope that this would offer some real direction for us, I went to meet him. He listened to my predicament, was professionally impressive, charming, and empathic. He agreed to see my son, saying that he would start by running some tests on his thyroid, adrenalin, and neurotransmitters. At last I felt that we had an integrated approach. My son was eager to go for nutritional help and took his supplements, including niacinamide and essential fatty acids, without any coercion from me. In retrospect, I can see how my son guided his whole treatment plan.

Although this seemed like progress, I was increasingly aware of how my own health was getting me down. I had been to a new doctor's practice earlier in the year with flu-like symptoms that seemed not to respond to any type of rest. I noticed I was lying on my bed in the afternoons and seemed to have no energy. When I went to see him, I told him about my symptoms and my son. No sooner were the words out of my mouth then he handed me a prescription for antidepressants and antibiotics. He told me the antidepressants would take some weeks to work and might cause some digestive problems. I did not even take the prescription to the chemist. Two or three weeks passed and I felt no better, and then realized I had developed some small blisters towards the base of my spine. I was scared now. Maybe I had shingles. I made another appointment to see the doctor. Within a couple of minutes he asked me how I was getting on with the antidepressants. I told him I hadn't taken them; that if I was suffering from depression it was reactive and not endogenous. He told me I was the worst kind of patient, in that I made my own diagnosis, and if I didn't do what he said there was no point in coming to see him. He was right, and I was right too.

Walking home from the surgery, I could feel my anger surging through my body. Somehow, in a weird way, it motivated me. I had to come to terms with the fact that I was stressed and that this was taking a physical toll on my body. Out of the dim recesses of my mind, I remembered learning a profound relaxation technique called Autogenics at a healing retreat. I had realized then that I had felt calmer and more centred with Autogenics than with any meditation I had practised. At the moment, I certainly couldn't meditate to save my life. I went home and looked it up on my good old friend, the Internet. This is what it said. "Autogenic Therapy is a self-help method which brings about profound relaxation and relief from the negative effects of stress. Autogenic means generated from within. The technique mobilises our innate systems for healing and recuperation." This was what I needed. Psychotherapy alone could not address the accumulated stress held in my physical body. Within a few days I had not only booked my eight one-hour sessions, I had enrolled for the one-year training.

Back at home, almost imperceptibly, we began to notice that my son was becoming more social and interactive. Was it true? Was he really getting better? I had high hopes of the orthomolecular approach. I remember one evening when we all sat in the garden having a barbeque. He was making jokes and laughing. Maybe, maybe, maybe our guest was about to make a final exit.

My daughter and her boyfriend, who had been with us for several months now, had also become acquainted with our uninvited guest. They felt, however, that things were improving slightly, and that they would like to return to their travels. I felt so guilty that I had asked them to come back in the first place. Not only that, but I had been miserable, self-absorbed, and tunnel-visioned throughout their stay. My daughter had been there for us both, but she deserved her life back. So they left for the halcyon white beaches of Mozambique, but I knew the pain never left her either.

And then something crucial happened. My son, who was still suffering from digestive problems, said he would like to see the acupuncturist who had helped him get over his post viral fatigue following glandular fever. I thought it could do no harm. I had studied a little bit about Chinese medicine in my training for Feng Shui many years before. The *Book of Nei Jing* is the handbook for the meridian lines used in acupuncture and was written five thousand years ago. This was ancient medicine and ancient wisdom that understood the way "chi energy" circulates in the body and how the flow can be improved with the use of fine needles. In Yorkshire, we had benefited from the work of a superb Japanese acupuncturist. She had seen us all through our family propensity to develop tonsillitis and sinusitis with astonishing success. Acupuncture had been our family friend.

My son came home from his first acupuncture appointment and announced that the professor had told him to stop taking so many supplements, because they were making his digestive problems worse. Too many cooks were now involved. Oh why, why had I agreed to this? There and then he stopped taking the recommended doses. I tried in vain to persuade him to start retaking the dosages prescribed. With absolute lucidity, he pointed out that I wasn't a doctor and that he chose to listen to the professor. And I had to just sit back and wait and watch, helpless and powerless and ridiculously wondering if I was overreacting. I was furious with myself, with the acupuncturist, with life. I realized that when we become an expert in a field, it can often close our minds to other avenues, no matter whether they are in the realm of conventional or complementary medicine. Damn, damn, damn. Maybe it would all come right.

In the background, the doctor of integrated medicine recommended a psychiatrist who, he assured me, was open to the orthomolecular approach and would be happy to offer me advice. I went to see him, alone, of course, as ever. My story is getting boring now; it is so repetitive. He said he would help me in whatever way he could, but unless I could get my son to visit him there was nothing he could do. If he saw him, he would prescribe conventional medication in conjunction with the integrative doctor's prescriptions for vitamin supplements. He asked me to keep in touch with him and let him know how things developed, which I regularly did. He, in turn, recommended me to a private doctor in Harley Street for my own health. I duly went to the hallowed, high-ceilinged room, where I met an attentive and sympathetic doctor. But when I told him about my son, the advice was the same as always. I had to wait for the situation to get worse.

And gradually, over the next few weeks, it did deteriorate. My son's healthy interest in his supplements and his nutritional programme began to wane. He was different; the air was different, somehow pregnant with despondent surrender.

One morning, I woke with a terrible crick in my neck. I couldn't look to the left or right, the searing pain in my neck heralding what my mind could not take in. And that was the day; the day when neither of us could manage any more. There were no extreme dramas, no violence, and no cataclysmic events, just a day too long. I called my ex to come down that very day. That awful surreal day I do not want to remember, another pale grey summer weekday of no particular significance to anyone else.

The following day, my son went to hospital.

One definition of a traumatic experience is that it literally robs one of one's speech. It is an experience that is unspeakable. I do not want to speak about it or write about it. I could write an entire book about it except that I don't know the words. My heart broke. My wonderful, darling son had a blameless illness and now was having this stigma-inducing experience. Like King Canute, I could not stop the tides of life itself. I was one broken human being that had to surrender to my own powerlessness in the workings of the universe.

And the system that operates in this country was put to the test. Suffice to say that getting help was made particularly difficult because he did not have a criminal record, had not committed a crime, and was not a risk to anyone or himself. My initial phone call to the crisis intervention team was made at four in the afternoon, and I was told they were all preparing to go home, and could I ring again in the morning; they were experiencing difficulty in getting beds at the moment. At least I was sharing the craziness with my ex. But we were both numb, both distressed, both lost, and trying somehow to help each other. In the end, out of desperation with the system, we used a private agency and a private hospital.

The deed was done, and I had to be strong. I had to visit the hospital and be solid and supportive and take him clean clothes and CDs. I had to keep going. Although I had my own private psychiatrist waiting in the wings, I had to go with the one that was randomly allocated to my son. I never met him. In private hospitals the psychiatrists make their visits in the evening after their NHS daytime job. He made a couple of telephone calls to me to confirm the diagnosis, etc., but that was all.

I liaised in the main with the very competent and affable male staff nurse. I asked the hospital to observe my son's dietary require-ments because of his allergies and took his vitamin supplements in with the dosage prescription exactly as before the acupuncture debacle. If I had taken in a small alien, the same amazed response might have been appropriate. The male staff nurse obviously thought I was some kind of nutritional nutcase. When I went on my next visit they were not in my son's room. I asked where they were, only to be told they had been locked in the poison cupboard and were not to be made available to my son on the orders of his psychi-atrist.

One day as I leave the hospital, I leave my son's room and head for the exit. I have to walk past the nurses' station. The bright, cheery, male staff nurse and the young female nurse look up from their station. They see the tears streaming down my face. They drop their eyes in unison and embarrassment. Through my watery vision, and my inherent training, I keep on watching them. Their eyes remain focused downwards. I recognize their lack of desire to be emotionally touched. I know for them total empathy in their job would be suicide. Nevertheless, I feel abandoned by them. My hunched gait alone carries my pain as I head for the door.

I am so mixed up. Part of me is relieved that my son is receiving care. Part of me hates to see him on the medication which makes him slow and dull. I feel as if I cannot look into his eyes; somehow, he is not quite there. The medication does not seem to be working the hoped-for miracle. He is on Olanzapine. Because it isn't working, they increase the dose. When it doesn't work again, they up the dose. When it still isn't working, they up the dose.

I pull rank with the psychiatrist treating my son. I get the psychiatrist waiting in the wings to call him and request that he allows the vitamin supplements to be taken. I ask him to explain that they are harmless and a valid treatment. I know I am being the worst kind of patient's mother. I know I am taking away the authority of my son's psychiatrist. But I care too much about the outcome to worry about his ego. I am truly astonished that no one seems to have heard of the forty-year-old orthomolecular psychiatric approach.

With my son in hospital I wonder whether I should take a break, but it seems inappropriate. Anyway, by this time I do not know what a break is. I continue seeing my clients. In the therapy hour I give my undivided attention to them. I realize how many of their lives have been coloured by mental illness, not just their own, but in their families and partners. They have no idea what I am going through. Worse than that, I have no idea what I am going through.

It is my regular Monday evening slot at college. I am sitting briefly in the therapists' waiting room. The secretary comes in to see me. She gives me back my dissertation on my weekend workshop and my two case studies. I have extremely high marks and there, nestling in the large brown envelope, is my Diploma and a note to say that I will be accredited that month with the UKCP. It doesn't feel like an achievement. My grey mantle now fits like a second skin.

I leave college at seven o'clock, but the warm, blue, sunny evening doesn't warm my heart. I gaze passively at the swans gliding along the canal. Nothing, even in nature, seems to register as pleasure. I had promised to ring my mother; she was going to see the doctor today because she hasn't been feeling good. She does not even know my son is in hospital. I call her; she tells me brightly, without any insight, that her doctor wants to speak to me urgently and has asked me to ring him the next morning between 9 and 10. I hurry home; I need to talk to my friend, Signor Pinot Grigio.

The next morning, when I wake, I cannot make sense of my experiences. Is it the Signor that has addled my brain? My son, my diploma, my work, oh, and I have to ring my mother's doctor. I ring from my bedroom. I am standing by the window. His familiar Yorkshire accent initially comforts me, and then he tells me my mother has Alzheimer type dementia. He says he wants me to go up and see her as soon as possible. Instantly and embarrassingly, the floodgates break open. I burst into noisy tears.

I lie on my bed sobbing. I have spent the last five years bemoaning my mother's depression and narcissism in therapy. The day I get my diploma, the universe deals one of its synchronistic cards that mark the first sign of her demise.

I stop crying. I make a plan. I can go and visit her for two nights while my son is in hospital. I put on my best suit of armour and visor. I pick up my pennant and prepare for the next round on my sturdy steed of habitual responses.

Reflections on surrendering

So, all the grim prophecies regularly given to me about waiting for my son to get seriously worse had come to pass. I had been in the unenviable position of waiting in the wings for "something" to happen. How awful that "something" might be had been left to play out in my imagination. But now I had to learn to accept that my fear of my son being hospitalized had become a reality. I had been a one-person audience watching a Greek tragedy unfold between the victim, my son, and the aggressor, none other than the then widely practised current interpretation of the Mental Health Act itself.

I had stood by and watched the crazy scene of our present mental health system unfold; only offering treatment to a first-episode sufferer either through the option of presenting their symptoms with the GP or by becoming a risk to themselves or others. Neither of these options had ever been available to us. My son would never have gone to the doctor with symptoms he did not know he had, nor did he ever present a risk to himself or others. The determining factor in my search for effective treatments was my son's health; treatment that we ultimately paid for privately in our desperation to get help. It felt that our journey through the illness had been made immeasurably more agonizing by the current mental health system. I now know I am not alone in these experiences.

> This difficulty, of getting treatment to begin, is a constant theme among carers. In a system driven by fear, which is only concerned with the prevention of violence, getting help for the merely ill, or distressed or disturbed is close to impossible. . . .
>
> The Act has also been widely misunderstood as providing for admission of patients only if there is a risk to their own or others' safety. In fact, the Act provides for admission in the interest of the patient's health or for his or her safety or for the safety of other people. The Code of Practice issued with the act in 1993 spelt this out clearly but it appears to have had little impact on practice. [Laurence, 2003, p. 160]

The "little impact on practice" was what I had gone through. My personal anguish through this period makes me feel the necessity to "beat my drum" once more with the observation that people in psychosis have no insight into their illness. Paradoxically, I do not feel like beating anything; it is I who feel beaten.

I believe the route of a first-episode patient with psychosis presenting themselves voluntarily to the GP or psychiatrist must be something of a rarity. Psychosis is not like other illnesses. The main presenting symptom is not the paranoid delusions, however bizarre and unpleasant they may be. The most dangerous delusion of all is that the person does not know they are ill. Someone in psychosis loses the ability to be self-referential. They no longer know how to act in their own best interests. They believe their beliefs; they do not see them as symptoms. They effectively lose their own voice.

It is left to those around them to recognize the warning signs as indicators of impending psychosis. It is the family or friends who observe the worsening or improvement of symptoms. In fact, to really understand the first-episode symptoms of someone, the consistent behaviour pattern of the personality has to have been known before. Aberrant personality traits can only be observed in the light of the knowledge of the usual personality.

It was this little discussed but predominating feature of the illness that made my own process so frustrating. Why are there no guidelines on how and where to register the warning and impending signs of psychosis? Am I alone in thinking like this? If my son had developed a grumbling appendix, would it have been acceptable to postpone treatment until it had become inflamed and infected, as in peritonitis, and become a life-threatening situation?

To take the analogy further: what if the peritonitis could only be recognized by a scar on the face? A scar that could only be seen by family, friends, and outsiders. What if the scar tissue was invisible to the sufferer themselves? An aberrant patch of skin they could neither physically feel nor see in a mirror. How would we best help the sufferer then? He can't see his own scar? Would we then wait until the scar tissue spreads to someone else, contaminates them, or harms them, before offering them treatment?

I need to state my position clearly here before it might appear that I am going into a rant about mental health professionals and care plans in general. I want to acknowledge the professionalism and care of many who have made their careers in psychiatry, social services, and mental health care. I have no desire to criticize a body of professional people who are, at source, a huge number of highly trained and skilled individuals with good hearts and intentions. However, the current system is woefully inadequate. Yet, I am encouraged to observe a sea change in the world of psychiatry; a growing recognition for the need for early intervention. At last, in some areas, there is a genuine move towards care at home, although currently this is may be geographically patchy. This movement towards more effective treatment is illustrated in the case study details on p. 89.

I am not quite sure how, or exactly when, we arrived at this place where the experiences of family and friends are virtually ignored in assessing a first episode. Before the 1960s, families were at liberty to cart their loved ones off to the local institution and leave them there for years on end. The rights of the psychotic individual were ignored, and they were left to the mercy of their families and the institutional world. Maybe the current situation is a backlash against those decades, marked by their failure to acknowledge the human rights of those diagnosed as mentally ill. Perhaps the blame for this disgraceful past has been laid at the door of families to the extent that their version of events is no longer considered trustworthy. Whatever the cause, it is vital that remedial action is taken.

As the situation presently exists, mental health professionals hold the only voice in treatment plans for psychotic patients. The patients have lost their voice. The family has lost theirs. At the present time, we are battling against the "story of illness that trumps all others in the modern period [that] of the medical narrative. The story told by the physician becomes the one against which all others are ultimately judged" (Frank, 1995, p. 5).

It is the medical profession alone that decides what is in the patient's best interest. Somehow, along the way, this system has developed as a way of protecting the individual rights of the patient and has succeeded in leaving families ignored.

Does the family not have the right to speak out for the patient, particularly at the beginning of a first episode when there is no mental health care team in place? It is family members or friends who first notice that the sufferer is losing conscious control of his reasoning faculties and innate sense of self. Nightmare qualities envelop the family as they fear for the well being of their relative. Not just any old fear, but the existential fears of suicide, violence, death, and murder. With the current interpretation of the Mental Health Act, waiting for dangerous situations to occur is nothing short of crazy and criminal for the patient, the family, and society.

So often are the family's cries for help ignored or rejected that it is hardly surprising that sectioning, frequently "attacked as a heavy-handed and intrusive instrument" (Laurence, 2003, p. 159), has turned into a lifeline for many families, as it too often marks the beginning of long overdue treatment.

For early intervention to become the reality the psychiatric profession wants it to be, then the treatment must involve the primary carer's voice, as an additional tool in the diagnostic procedure. The situation of a simple liaison between patient and mental health professional is only part of a complex picture of the patient's condition.

Psychotic behaviour is erratic. Patients are not psychotic all the time. They move in and out of consensus reality, watch television, make tea, and talk about the news. They can actually become quite adept at trying to cover their tracks. It is difficult sometimes to nail the exact time when the patient will move into aggression.

One client eventually got an outreach home visit from the psychiatrist for her son, who had been intermittently violent and aggressive. When the psychiatrist called, her cleaner was round with her little boy. Her son was sitting on the settee with the young child, playing computer games and being very kind to the child. Ironically, it looked more like an advert for children's TV than the menacing reality that lurked in the background. The psychiatrist agreed to come back in three days to reassess the situation. The mother's voice and story of the violence was ignored until the psychiatrist could see it for himself, even though her safety had been severely threatened.

The following case studies highlight an urgent need for change in the development of early intervention and outreach programmes. They also illustrate the psychological traumatic experience of witnessing "sectioning".

Case study one (2007)

> After two years of violent and harrowing experiences, Yvonne feels she has a fantastic support team for her son, Sam. Previously to this, on separate occasions, he had smashed the kitchen window and attacked the television with a baseball bat. She had had to call the police out three times. The first time they took him to A&E; he did a runner. The second time they decided he wasn't dangerous enough. After the third police visit, they tell her to visit her GP. The next day she goes to visit a different GP. Rules have been changed. The GP can now directly contact the Crisis Mental Health Team at the hospital. The GP comes round the next day with two psychiatrists, and a psychiatric nurse. They bring medication. For the next three months, two nurses come each day to make sure Sam takes the drugs. He is also assigned a psychologist, who visits once a week. After the three-month period, the

psychologist still visits once a week. He is a cool dude, intelligent and caring who supports Sam in taking his medication.

Sam is never sectioned. The combination of calling the police out and being a first-episode sufferer in the system qualified him for this admirable care package. After two years of hell, with no support or medication, Yvonne now feels that she cannot thank the hospital enough. Sam does not work, and is still taking recreational drugs, and is far from integrated into society, but she feels supported by the team and attends Carers Liaison Meetings at his hospital.

Case study two (2007)

Elaine is extremely anxious. John has been having psychotic episodes for seven years. He has taken himself off medication for several weeks and is now showing signs of aggression. As his regular psychiatric assessment is due, Elaine, who is extremely concerned about him, accompanies him. He is agitated, picking at imaginary things on his body and mumbling to himself.

During the consultation, the psychiatrist, realizing that John is not well, persuades him to agree to a voluntary hospital admission. Elaine is hugely relieved. They wait in the waiting room. The psychiatrist comes back and tells them that, unfortunately, there are no beds. It is 5.00 p.m. and there is nothing they can do. He advises them to come back in the morning.

Elaine asks what is she to do if he gets worse, aggressive. They tell her to take him to A&E. She drives away with John. She is unsure whether to drive straight to the hospital, turning left at the crossroads, or to go right and drive home. At the junction in the traffic jam, she indicates left. John realizes she is going to the hospital and pulls the steering wheel away from her. Immediately, she hears all the cars hooting around her. She says to John, "We are going to the hospital." He bangs her head against the car window and she swerves the car again, amid more hoots from the early evening traffic jam.

She knows now she has got to drive to the hospital no matter what. She walks straight to the front of the A&E queue and tells them it is an emergency. They tell her there is a four-hour wait. She tells them they cannot wait that length of time. They give John a tranquillizer and put them both back out into the waiting room. For four hours they sit there, with John going out every ten minutes for a fag. Elaine doesn't know each time he goes out whether he will come back.

Eventually, after a diagnosis, they report there are no NHS beds available. Another two hours later, John is transferred by ambulance to a private mental health hospital. Elaine is hugely relieved that at last he is getting treatment, but furious at the crazy way she had to get it.

Case study three (2003)

Bob comes to his first therapy session. He wants to talk about his "Nemesis": he believes he will have to pay for his past actions.

When he was eight, he watched his mother attack his father with a knife. It was then he realized she was ill. She was diagnosed with schizophrenia. She was taken away. For a long period following, he spent most of his weekends visiting her in various mental institutions. He described his childhood experiences of watching people out of control of their own lives, interned and drugged up. Thus began a life-long fear of it happening to him.

When he was twenty-five, he had been responsible for having his mother sectioned. She had been sectioned three times in the previous five years, but this was the first time he had been solely responsible. On the other occasions, his brother and sister had been present. Watching six policemen bundle her into a van had left him feeling that he had sacrificed her for his own mental well being. Worse than that, he believed he drove people mad.

He felt that he could not get on with his life because he feared that some kind of retributive justice would punish him for his actions. Even though it happened over ten years ago, the memory still haunts him.

Case study four (2008)

Ava, aged forty-six, lives at home with her younger brother Douglas (forty-four). He has been psychotic for almost four years now. He has had no treatment whatsoever. She describes it as living on a rollercoaster. Douglas believes that there is absolutely nothing wrong with him. It is the government that is curtailing his life and recording all his phone calls. He is paranoid about being watched. He doesn't visit the GP for any reason at all. He sees the doctor as "having records on him".

Life is agonizing for Ava. She lives in constant fear. She says at home her heart pounds so hard she wonders if he can hear it thumping; even if things are not that bad, her heart pounds. She describes her brother's responses as vacillating between toxic silence and a tsunami of fury.

She wants to leave and go and live on her own, but the more isolated she feels her brother becomes, the more she needs to be the one who does not desert him. She feels torn between being locked out of his thoughts and beliefs and being vitriolically accused by him of causing satanic freakery in the home.

She feels unable to get help because her brother categorically denies that he has problems. He lacks insight and is paranoid. He would view any form of medical record as a state conspiracy to gather information. She has no idea what to do.

Case study five (2008)

Marina has had to give up on her forty-three year old son, who has been psychotic for twenty-six years. He has been hostile, incoherent, and downright difficult since he was seventeen. He is so disruptive that all the half-way houses have refused to admit him, so he is now a voluntary in-patient. He goes out each day, returning to the ward to sleep. She has tried over the years to be kind to him. At the last lunch, he demanded money for drugs; as soon as she gave it to him, he left the restaurant. She wants to help him but feels she has hit a brick wall, but talking about it reminds her that she never gets over her guilt. Last week, she had a letter from the hospital saying that he had been sectioned for the seventeenth time. She said they all go through the motions. She says wistfully she wishes there was a proper cure.

Different stories told by different people with different treatments available to them, but no cure in sight.

Meanwhile, I was having to deal with my own reactions to my son being in hospital. Strong denial, rather than shame, springs to mind. I felt very alone and told very few people. I felt most able to be honest and open with the ongoing support group we had formed from the workshop. It was from them I could receive support without feeling pitied. With those with no shared experience, I was extremely guarded and defensive. My ability to admit to myself what was happening was also limited.

To recap, my psychotherapy training had led me to understand that our minds are largely driven by unconscious processes outside of our awareness. Yet, our sense of self-identification is solely with our conscious mind, thoughts, and beliefs. This is our persona, our carefully constructed conscious self-image of how we want the world to see us and how we want to perceive ourselves.

My persona before the illness had been of a normal, polite, intelligent, affable person who, at best, was elegant and witty. My social construct was that I was a decent, law-abiding member of society, and my family construct was that I was the mother of two well-adjusted, successful, intellectual adult children, etc., etc. Dealing with my son's psychosis had already shattered many of the ideas I had about who I was. The hospitalization took away even more.

Part of my persona, my sophisticated, casually elegant, witty designer self, now lay at the back of the wardrobe like some old ball gown I would never fit into again. Raw experiences, raw pain, took me to new levels of my being. The person who walked past the nurses' station with tears streaming down her face no longer matched my narrow and false self image. I no longer had a continual set of masks to hide my distress. My affable self was nowhere to be seen.

The goal of many psychotherapeutic models is to heal the split between the conscious mind (the persona) and the unconscious mind (the shadow) and to achieve an integrated mind. An integrated mind helps people to be in touch with all of their mind rather than living solely with the persona and its automatic behaviour patterns. Changing unwanted habitual response patterns is one of the main reasons people enter psychotherapy.

The mystery lies in that no one yet understands how the conscious mind chooses which bits are unacceptable to its self-image and lobs them off into the vast reservoirs of the unconscious through splitting off, repression, denial, or projection. I realize now that I had unconsciously projected on to my son's first therapist my anger and despondency. My own rage and despair with my life was simply too uncomfortable to acknowledge. Taking personal responsibility for my own feelings through my therapy, I was just starting to integrate some of these shadowy aspects of myself.

However, I could not make sense of the way my psyche was operating. I felt that my self-image had taken rather too much of a battering. But that was only part of what was happening to me. The accumulation of stress in my body was now sending me too many symptoms of physical distress for me to ignore it any longer.

For several months now, for three weeks out of four, I had low-grade flu symptoms and a permanently husky voice. I could hide my flu symptoms, but all my friends could hear my throat, and would comment on it. It did not dawn on me that my body might be faithfully expressing my "lack of voice". On top of that, my digestion was poor, my abdomen was constantly bloated. No amount of careful eating or supplements could get rid of it. I slept with my shoulders up by my ears, as if they were earrings. My face was grey and drawn, my eyes tired and lifeless.

By this time, mercifully, I was several months into my training as an autogenic therapist. Here, I was learning, teaching, and prac-tising a mind–body therapy specifically designed to reduce stress. In retrospect, I think it saved me from cracking under the strain, both psychologically and physically.

Interestingly, autogenic therapy (AT) was developed by a psychiatrist and a peer of Freud's. Johannes Schultz was a profes-sor of neuropsychiatry in Germany in the 1920s and 1930s, where he was at the forefront of mind–body medicine. He had been a student of Oskar Vogt, who was a neuropathologist. Vogt was involved in research on hypnosis, and observed that patients who had been subjected to conventional forms of hypnosis experienced remarkable relief from tension and fatigue.

The remarkable thing about holding tension in our bodies, as I was, for instance, in my shoulders, is that these blocks happen to us. We do not consciously make them happen. These tension blocks serve a significant function, just like the psychological defence mechanisms of the mind; they stop us feeling. They are forms of resistance to dangerous emotions and impulses, such as sup-pressed, held-in anger or rage. By the same token, although every skeletal muscle is under voluntary control, we are not consciously able to make them relax. We need to be able to access the involun-tary and unconscious systems of the body, such as circulation, heart rate, respiration, etc., to be able to exert any influence on them.

Schultz drew on these observations, but, in his genius ap-proach, designed a self-hypnosis technique for people to be able to induce a deep mental and psychological relaxation at will rather than at the behest of the hypnotist. Autogenic therapy, meaning self-generating, was born. Schultz devised an auto suggestion technique which establishes mental contact with the body's involuntary processes. This enables the body to switch from the sympathetic response of "stressed out" to the parasympathetic response of "chilled out", resulting in profound psychophysical relaxation. Until then, the discovery of the autogenic, the autonomic nervous system, had been considered beyond the realm of conscious control.

Throughout my psychotherapy training I had been working towards integrating the unconscious processes in my mind. Now I was starting to look at integrating the unconscious processes in my body and to acknowledge my total psychophysical self, not just with my mind, but through feeling attention to my body.

I learnt how over-identified we are with our mind and its thought processes. The conscious mind can only identify with the voluntary processes of the body. It can only say, I take a deep breath, or I bend my knees. It cannot say, I beat my heart, or I am digesting the egg. Yet, in every second of our life, our total organism of mind and body, without any help from the mind, is "coordinating literally millions of processes at once, from the intricacies of digestion to the complexities of neurotransmission" (Wilber, 2001, p. 106).

Put another way, we behave as if beneath our mind our body just dangles away, doing its own thing. The consequence of this means that we have come to believe that there is a radical split between our mind and body. While the mind has us in its grip, we can live in a constant state of anxiety without ever thinking about the effects on our bodies. The reality is, however, that mental and physical well being actually circulate in one continuous process in the psychophysical organism.

What is interesting, in retrospect, about my training in autogenic therapy was that not one of my fellow colleagues at my psychotherapy college had heard of it. Just as, I suspect, you may have not heard of it. My instinct to follow up my earlier experience had come about as just a dredge of a memory, but with some sort of insistence on action. Somehow, I had been drawn invisibly to it.

Because of my autogenic training, I cannot buy into the concept of a mental disorder being a biological or pathological brain disorder. Autogenic therapy showed me clearly that it is possible to influence physiological processes thought to be automatic and not susceptible to voluntary intervention. The idea of merely correcting chemical imbalances in the brain as if it was separate from the body could not be possible. Like many before me, I have come to the conclusion that the bias in Western thought that the mind is totally in the head and a function of the brain needs to be abandoned.

To understand mental illness, we have to understand ourselves as a total psychophysiological organism. The unconscious does not just reside in the psyche, unconscious memory is stored in every cell in the body. It stands to reason, therefore, that although psychosis may primarily be a psychological breakdown or seen as an extreme defence mechanism of the unconscious mental processes; it must have accompanying physical symptoms. The very often unpleasant thought processes that accompany psychosis must produce physical reactions associated with stress, if not trauma, causing all manner of symptoms like fatigue and poor digestion.

Psychoneuroimmunology (PNI) is the study of the connections between the mind and the neural, immune, and endocrine hormonal systems that confirms the theory of the total psychophysiological organism. Perhaps PNI offers an easier way of understanding the hugely complex array of both physically and emotionally distressing psychological symptoms we witness in our loved ones.

*   *   *

Postscript one

I have been away for a few days writing this chapter. I have just arrived home from a long drive. It is late afternoon and I am going out to a fiftieth birthday party. My close friend and her partner are picking me up. We are friends now, but we share psychosis in the family. We speak on the phone at 5 p.m.; we agree to meet for a drink before the party at eight. An hour later, my mobile goes. My friend says she has just had a phone call from her son. He has been off the depot injections for three months now. Since then, she has been living on a knife edge, knowing that he is sliding gradually into the abyss. Tonight she knows he is right on the edge. He has been screaming at her, threatening and abusing her. She says to me, "Is this the day, the day I blow the whistle, the day he goes to hospital again?" At that point, she tells me her mobile is ringing and that it is the Emergency Duty Social Worker (EDSW). She hangs up.

I am tired, and the first half of the contents of this chapter about how the impact of the interpretation of the Mental Health Act affects families is still uppermost in my mind. Ninety minutes pass, and my friend rings back. The EDSW has told her that no action can be taken because her son is not suicidal. She is beside herself. This is not a one-day event. His condition has been deteriorating for at least a month. If he does nothing, she tells the EDSW, then he may be responsible for someone being harmed, and that someone could be her. The EDSW says that, in an emergency, she can always go to A&E or call the police. He tells her to give him a call on Monday. By that time she is screaming at him that there is no way she could possibly get her six-foot-four, aggressive, sixteen-stone son to A&E against his will, and that she will probably not be in a position to call the police if attacked.

At this point her partner comes home. He is an eminent solicitor. He takes over the phone call. He is logical, cool, and reasonable. Then, inflamed by the lack of response, he too finds himself raising his voice and getting angry. My friend says to me, we are both intelligent, reasonable people trying to do our best for my son. She is distraught, she doesn't drink much, but says she is on her third whisky. She describes the situation as "fucking insane".

I wonder about the tone of the first half of the chapter I had written earlier. I wonder about the reasonableness of my tone. I remember how cross I got at the logical and detached attitude of the books designed to help me. It is the last thing I planned to do but my friend's impassioned message of the "fucking insanity" of the system has to be acknowledged in some way.

It is true, the system can be morally wrong. It often does not act in the patient's best interest, which is insane and inhumane. Bring on James Laurence and his book *Pure Madness: How Fear Drives the Mental Health System* (2003). Is anybody listening?

The synchronicity between this evening's events and my writing on trying to get help from mental health teams leaves me overwhelmed. I cancel going to the party.

CHAPTER SIX

The wounded storyteller

Diary extract

It is hard to go on holding the telephone next to my ear. The tone of my mother's voice upsets me so. However, her fiercely independent, authoritarian self gives way as she tells me she cannot manage her paperwork any more. I am dealing with mine none too well at this point, but I dismiss that from my mind. I am trying to make arrangements to go and see how her dementia is impacting on her everyday life. "So you want to come and stay in my house?" she says, in a superior manner that reminds me of Hyacinth Bucket and implies that we are not related in any way. Although I may be poised on my white charger and wearing my familiar suit of armour, there is a new me in there; the hugely irritated, put down, and short-fused me.

Dealing with my mother's depression and her overt hostility was what unknowingly drove me to train as a psychotherapist. Now she is seventy-nine, and for the first time requires real assistance. Part of me childishly still wants her to need me on some level. She had certainly never needed my presence in the past except to offload her huge disappointment with life.

She saw her life as a great tragedy. She pretended her first husband of five years never existed, even though he was my father. He was unmentionable. Her main story featured around her becoming a widow nineteen years earlier from her second marriage, which she espoused as true love and devotion, but regrettably childless. Thus, she gave her depression legitimacy, an explanation, a story. Now, even at her great age, she was still hoping to meet a man who would take all her troubles away. The fantasy of finding a wonderful man occupied much of her thinking. This was what she wanted, and I was of no interest. She bemoaned endlessly her sense of isolation and defended against it by withdrawing from life even more. Her medical history was peppered with numerous visits to the doctors, who would repeatedly prescribe antidepressants. Sometimes, she would go as far as getting the prescription, but she would never take them for more than a day, saying the side-effects were too strong.

I was probably in my late thirties, with not a glimmering of understanding of psychotherapy, when I realized that she suffered from something that was more than just minor depression. We lived in a small village then, next to the church. Life seemed pretty perfect. I had two lovely children and a husband and was enjoying life. A local teenage girl used to help us out with babysitting. One Christmas Eve, while the babysitter's family was at Midnight Mass, the sitter's father hung himself in the stairwell. The magic of Christmas morning wiped out forever by that swinging noose and lifeless body. Some stories stay with us forever, and somehow that one does with me. It seemed particularly chilling as our Christmas had seemed so magical. I was truly shaken to the core by this tragedy happening so close to us. I felt for that beautiful young girl who had in some way become part of my family too.

Some days later, on the telephone, I told my mother about it, hoping she would lend a sympathetic ear to my sense of horror and shock. She was vitriolic and biting. She said it was disgraceful and criminal of the family not to have saved him. That I needed to change my attitude to life, that I should be accusing them and not sympathizing with them. My blood ran cold that day. I felt that the implicit message was that I should save her. I, in turn, was furious with her. I knew somehow that she was ill, but I kept her distorted perceptions to myself. Her lack of empathy and viciousness left me feeling deeply ashamed. I buried it deep within me as a dark secret.

So, the strange thing now about receiving her diagnosis of Alzheimer's type dementia was that it actually gave me some prospect of getting help for her. Maybe now, when at last she had a proper psychiatric illness, I might also be able to get her on some medication for her depression. Depression being loosely defined here, as her thinking and perceptions selectively perceived the world as negative and failed to perceive the positive. She had spent her whole life suffering, some times being better than others. Not for me was the worry that the diagnosis of dementia would turn my sweet, gentle, elderly mother into a harridan. The reverse was actually true. I hoped that her angry, punitive nature would evaporate and reveal a sweet little old lady, the mother I had always yearned for. She had never gone for the old lady look in any way. Her outstanding natural beauty as a Jackie Onassis look-alike, with thick auburn hair and smart clothes, was still how she presented herself to the world.

But that was her external image. Her inner world, unfortunately, had never presented itself as quite ill enough to receive psychiatric care. Like many others of that generation, she battled alone with her depression without recourse to medication or psychological support. Through my work as a therapist, I increasingly became aware of this very common phenomenon of people falling just outside psychiatric crisis care management. Even though we appear to live in a world of easily available antidepressants, there are many people who struggle with severe mental health issues without any recognition.

When I arrived at my mother's bungalow, where she had lived for the past thirty-five years, its familiarity blinded me to seeing it as another private mental hospital for one. Nothing external looked amiss. The garden, the love of her life, was immaculate, mature, and a delight to the eye and the senses. The interior of the house could not have changed. That was another aspect of her illness. She could not change anything. I think a TV interiors programme could use her home as an example of how houses looked in 1970. Everything was original to that date, including the fridge and the cooker. The turquoise embossed carpet in the living room was still pristine, as no sunlight was ever allowed to fade its vibrant pile.

She herself was still as sharp as a barrowload of monkeys. In her isolated existence, which was her favourite phrase, she was dealing efficiently with her gradual loss of memory. She wrote absolutely everything down. But there was a kind of missing of connections. She told me of going to visit the memory clinic as if it was afternoon tea at the Ritz. She said it was a special place for single, elderly, retired people to go, because everybody at her age started to lose their memory. I marvelled at the capacity of her defence mechanisms to weave an acceptable narrative around what, basically, were visits to the Elderly Mentally Ill unit.

However, she didn't like the consultant at the memory clinic. She felt demeaned by the experience. I pause here: do I tell the truth? I think of the power of untold stories. My mother, in part, did not like the consultant because she was not white. That is the truth of it. She was deeply suspicious of all foreigners, and always had been. In these cross-culturally enlightened times, embarrassingly for me and deeply shaming (yet another one of my secrets), my mother was xenophobic. I can cope with it a little better than I used to be able to because I now realize it is often just a product of that particular generation and the narrow times in which they lived. For our minds are shaped not just by our families, but the times we live in, and the cultural and social aspects of those times.

My mother-in-law, too, was shaped in this way. She had been in hospital, aged ninety-nine and three quarters, with terminal cancer, her hundredth birthday only weeks away. One day, she had asked for a white nurse to change her. This caused absolute and understandable mayhem. The nurse reported her, and the result was that she was officially reprimanded by the hospital administrative team and given a warning. A repeat episode and she would be asked to leave the hospital and also face a tribunal. Illness of any form means not just dealing with the illness, but dealing with the rules of the hospital system. Her forthcoming appointment in the next few weeks with the Grim Reaper and St Peter stood for nought next to the hospital rules.

I am aware at this point of how important our stories are. I am surprised at which ones leap into my mind. Stories I thought I had forgotten, yet they appeared, seemingly unbidden yet pertinent and illustrating what I would be unable to put into words. These small stories formed part of a larger whole, shaping me and moulding me along the way. In the telling of these stories, what I am doing is introducing you to the hugely difficult personality traits and behaviour patterns, including overt racism, I was going to have to deal with in my mother. I am trying to lay the foundation stones to describe how her mental illness often drove me to despair and tested the very limits of my endurance, even though in my heart I loved her desperately.

Anyway, "Jim'll fix it" was the persona I adopted for the new experience of being able to help her. For the first time in my adult life, I was allowed into the locked back bedroom, the study, and the piles and piles of paper and her precious finances. By this time she could not throw any pieces of paper away. She had always been extremely secretive, so I was not allowed to pick anything up unless she gave permission. I had bought some transparent file boxes. I did everything in her presence. I wrote everything down. I filed the bills and the receipts. I wrote clear labels on everything. I wrote down exactly what I had done and why in the form of a letter to her, in case she forgot she had asked me to do it. I promised I would go regularly and help her.

Along with everything else, she thought that she might have a brain tumour and that this was causing the memory problems. This, of course, had been the cause of my stepfather's death. I was trying to plan ahead for her and help her. Thankfully, I knew my mother still had private health insurance. It was the only thing she spent any money on as a result of my encouragement and a hang-over from when my stepfather was still alive. Otherwise, minimum expenditure was still the order of the day, as if wartime rationing was still operational.

I made a call to her private health insurance company to ask what we could claim for. She had been paying an exorbitant prem-ium because of her age all these years and never claimed anything. The phone person told me that there was a ceiling limit of £2000 allocated per year for mental health care on my mother's policy. However, they could not pay out anything for Alzheimer's type dementia, or depression. Not being able to claim for my mother's mental illness on the health insurance became just another step in my growing awareness of the general differences and attitudes between trying to get help for a mental illness rather than a physi-cal illness.

I immersed myself in being busy with my mother's problems. This offered a brief respite from my aching heart. I spoke to the doctor. He was arranging a brain scan. I told him of the difficulty with the consultant at the memory clinic. I braced myself and told him the true reason. He was very understanding, and said he would help as much as he could in finding someone else. I clambered back on the train to London. I had done as much as I could. It was now time to prepare for the aftercare programme at our private mental health hospital number one.

But now I had only the dimmest awareness that I was almost totally running on autopilot, with my feelings buried somewhere in between my grey mantle and my tightly fitting armour. Of course, just like every other phase of the illness, not one person gave me any clue of what to expect. They were all first experiences.

When I went to pick up my son from hospital, the male nurse proudly told me that he had been a model patient and had caused no trouble at all. I think he thought this was down to them and the medication. This brought me no comfort. This was his personality, the person he was at heart. I think it is important for people to know that psychosis does not always have to be viewed as violent or disruptive.

My son could not wait to get out of the hospital. When I asked him about his interactions with the hospital psychiatrist there, he described him as obviously having no idea what it felt like to be the patient. He described him as talking to him as if he was giving a truck driver verbal instructions on how to learn to swim. I marvel at that analogy; I could not think of a phrase that could better describe a lack of genuine interaction. "Verbal Instructions on How to Swim for Truck Drivers." That wouldn't be making the bestseller list.

But I didn't feel quite as alone as before. The integrative psychiatrist had been quietly waiting in the wings to take over his case and, the very day my son came out of hospital, he went for his first consultation. I had always visited him alone in the past. He changed his medication immediately to Abilify (Aripiprazole), which at that time was a new medication. He also continued his orthomolecular prescriptions. Within three days any lingering symptoms of psychosis had disappeared and he was less sedated. I was pleased. Maybe it would all soon be over. I was always looking for the nightmare to end. I soon realized London was no place for convalescence. My son needed fresh air and nature and so did

I. By the end of the week we were heading up to Yorkshire, to a country cottage amid fields and trees and the support of his father.

I was pleased with the new medication, but I was pleased too soon. When we got to our cottage, the side-effects of the medication really began to kick in. His whole nervous system responded with restlessness in his arms and legs. Thank God, we were in the country. He walked and plodded and plodded and walked in order to minimize the discomfort he was in. He found it almost impossible to sit down. His distress was palpable. It was difficult to know what to do. I called the psychiatrist, but he advised that my son's body needed to learn to tolerate the drug, especially because any other symptoms had disappeared. I trusted him implicitly. It sounded good sense and we had no other options. So my ex and I just had to watch without being able to help our son's huge physical discomfort and reactions to the drugs. But, somehow, we are all hard wired to deal sympathetically with physical pain we can observe rather than inner mental distress. And the main thing was, he was our son again, and that was all that mattered for now.

One early evening, alone, I went to visit my mother. It was a beautiful summer's evening, if one can describe the weather as an external event divorced from the feelings in our hearts. She was in the garden in shorts and a sunhat. She invited me in for a drink. She seemed not to be able to grasp at all what was going on in my life, even though part of her script would include, "How are the children?" I was resigned to it. I didn't really want to talk about it anyway; it was too upsetting.

We went inside the house, which seemed dark in contrast to the bright sunshine outside. Maybe it was the sudden change from light to dark that caused the monster to leap out from the shadows. It was the fiendish and dragon-like part of my mother. Flames metaphorically flaring from her nostrils, she started verbally to assassinate me. "How dare you interfere with my private papers. How dare you touch my belongings!" All the files I had bought for her were piled up neatly on the dining table, minus their invoices and receipts. She told me to take them away immediately, that I was untrustworthy, and under no circumstances was I ever to talk to her doctor about her again. She might be losing her memory but it seemed not to be letting her down right now. She was as fierce as ever. These were not new symptoms; this was a consistent pattern of her behaviour that I recognized and knew intimately. I tried in vain to defend myself. She demolished me by telling me I was lying. I lost every gram of patience or understanding for her illness that I might have gleaned along the way. Every bit of my therapist nature deserted me. I picked up the box files and walked straight out. The four-year-old in me slammed the door for good measure. For the rest of my stay in Yorkshire, I went nowhere near her; my priority was my son. I had abandoned my aged, ill mother. It didn't make me feel good, but I could not cope with the abuse while I felt so low.

Back at the convalescent cottage, the physical side-effects of the muscle fasciculation for my son continued and continued. Each day we waited patiently for it to abate. It was difficult to focus on anything else at this stage, as the muscle spasms were so intense. The long drive back to London became a serious source of concern. Would he be able to manage the journey? I had to call our psychiatrist, who sent us a prescription for a muscle relaxant to counteract these side-effects. We were starting on the well-known bandwagon of taking more drugs to combat the side-effects of other drugs, but this was how it had to be. With the help of the secondary drugs, the restlessness abated enough for us to travel home, but it was an anxious drive. Oh, that we could put all this behind us. But there was absolutely no way we could leave this illness behind.

Once home, there were new precipices to climb. The accompanying classic by-products of psychosis are anxiety and depression; those minor little symptoms now had to be dealt with. These, of course, had become well-ingrained, habitual responses to the altered states of consciousness which my son had endured for years. Because the mental health system only caters for emergencies that involve life or death situations, it perpetuates the accompanying symptoms of anxiety and depression until they are very difficult to get over.

In one respect we were now very fortunate in the care my son was receiving, even if it was so horribly overdue. We had a great psychiatrist and, by this time, a wonderful GP: a GP who told me that the trick with medicine was to combine the best of the NHS with private medicine, and the best of conventional medicine with complementary medicine. I wished he ran a national training school for doctors. My son was on an absolute medley of medication for all his symptoms and the side-effects of the medication. There was no way I was waving my alternative banner now. They were necessary and life saving. He also continued with the ortho-molecular supplements. In retrospect, it was a wonder he could do anything else all day besides pop tablets.

As time went by and some of the side-effects began to diminish, he went for cognitive–behaviour therapy (CBT). This is a short-term therapy treatment that is designed to alter thinking patterns through goals and action plans. Specifically, it was through this approach that my son learnt to tolerate his own anxiety. He would be set weekly tasks to complete that were designed to push the boundaries and limits of his anxiety. CBT is based on the assump-tion that most unwanted thinking patterns and emotional and behavioural reactions are learned over a long period of time. "Roger, Roger, Earth to Mars"—the longer the symptoms of psychosis are left without treatment the harder the anxiety and depression is to remove.

Months went past. The illness dominated our lives with its myriad complications, both physical and mental. Eventually, my son was referred to a day centre to rehabilitate him into society. Here he spent his days with other suffering human souls. These were a bunch of people who had faced life's vicissitudes through a number of ways. Although there were no fellow travellers from the psychosis camp, there were heroin addicts, alcoholics, drug dealers, anorexics, and transvestites. Our days were now full of stories of the day centre, as they once had been of university. My idea of what was normal had by this time totally slipped from view. Any personas I had previously adopted lay useless in the bin.

The journey of traversing up the mountain of total recovery from psychosis felt arduous and treacherous. It was made all the more lonely because there seemed to be no other travellers to cheer us on to the summit of a cure. The mountain was dotted with people in white coats brandishing small bottles of tablets. They believed the mountain was beyond being conquered. Looking towards the top of the mountain, I could not even see a cheerful flag fluttering in the breeze to mark the cured one's ascent. It made for a bleak view.

Reflections on the wounded storyteller

I had been invited away for a weekend in the country. A friend who was currently doing her MA in Creative Writing and Personal

Development at Sussex University wondered if I would like to go to the Lapidus Annual Conference. I had never heard of Lapidus. She told me it was a writing conference called "Writing Bodies, Reading Minds, Creating Our Identities", for both aspiring and published writers, and that there would be lots of experiential workshops to attend. I protested that I was not a writer, even though the seed of this book was implanted deep within me after writing up my weekend workshop. But a weekend in the country, the first in a very long time, was too luring a prospect to turn down.

Lapidus turned out to be an organization that promotes healing and personal growth through writing and reading; personal growth being loosely defined as the consciously applied intention to change aspects of one's own life. In some ways, it overlapped with the goals of psychotherapy itself. However, when I arrived at the opening dinner, I felt a fraud; I had not written anything other than course work. I looked around at what I imagined to be a sea of assured, polished, published, writing faces. In my ignorance of who was whom, and without registering my friend's raised eyebrows, I sat myself next to a highly acclaimed poet and author. When she later asked me what I had written, I feebly muttered into the apple crumble something about my dissertation. I really wondered what on earth I was doing there. I had nothing in print.

Throughout my training, I had been committing my own personal journey to paper for six or seven years now, but the quality of the narrative was secondary to therapeutic insights. In writing the case studies, I had not even realized I had been narrating other peoples' stories. I also had not considered my work as a psychotherapist as being a professional listener to stories. Writing my personal myth and my dissertation had brought personal insights, but all these seemed a very haphazard and tenuous link to understanding the importance of storytelling and the actual process of writing itself.

On the Saturday morning, there was a general presentation. I sat close to my friend and her fellow students, and fondly imagined I might look like one of them; at least they were unpublished as yet. A presenter called Andrew Sparkes was giving a talk on "Men, Sport and Spinal Cord Injury". I could not imagine what relevance this could possibly have for me and my work. He spoke of working with sportspeople who had suffered spinal cord injuries and had become paraplegic. His clients were people whose fitness levels were a prerequisite for their professional lives. He cited an example of a young professional rugby player running on to the Saturday tournament pitch, his toned muscular physique in the peak of perfect health. An hour later, he was carried off on a stretcher, paralysed and immobile. This was a powerful and heart wrenching image; perfect physique to instant immobility for someone whose physical prowess was their career. He explained that the natural tendency on hearing this story is to focus on the paralysis and loss of bodily control as the main feature of the tragic accident. However, the presenter pointed out that suffering involves whole persons, including both their mind and their body, at the very centre of which lies the "Wounded Storyteller".

Then, on the overhead projector, I saw his first slide. Instantly, he had all my attention.

> Seriously ill people are wounded not just in body but in voice. They need to become storytellers in order to recover the voices that illness and its treatment often takes away. *The Wounded Storyteller* by Arthur W. Frank. [1995, p. xii]

The presenter explained how his work had been influenced by Frank, whose central tenet was that the suffering experienced in illness creates a need for stories. Ill people need to tell their stories in order to construct new maps and new perceptions of their changing relationships to the world.

Drawing on Frank's theories, he described how newly disabled patients would find one of three different narrative structures, or general storylines, as they strove to tell their revised stories that would include their new-found suffering. The first one was the "Restitution Narrative" (*ibid.*, pp. 75–96), in which the person wanted to become healthy again and believed that the medical model would restore their health. The restitution plot had the basic storyline, "Yesterday I was healthy, today I'm sick, but tomorrow I'll be healthy again." The second storyline was the "Chaos Narrative", (*ibid.*, pp. 97–114), this being the opposite of restitution; its plot imagines life never getting better. The defining feature of chaos stories is that they have no narrative order. They are the stories of the victim and the consequent experiences of vulnerability, futility, and impotence. The third storyline was the "Quest Narrative" (*ibid.*, pp. 115–136), where the person meets their suffering head on and seeks to learn and use the experience. The quest narrative affords the ill person a voice as teller of his/her own story, because it is only in quest stories that the *teller* has a story to tell.

I am blown away by the lecture. I cannot buy the book, on sale in the foyer, quick enough. I no longer feel like an outsider at the conference. I feel that Frank has given me the insight to find a narrative for my own experiences. His inspiration for his book had come from his own battle with cancer, described as "an experience medicine cannot describe" (*ibid.*, p. 18). I know instantly that I want to translate his theories on the narrative of illness into the world of mental health. But still I worry whether my idea is valid or not.

Later on that day, I go for my appointment for free guidance on publishing proposals and publishers. I tentatively tell the young Scottish girl about my idea to write about my experiences of watching my son suffer psychosis and its treatment. I wonder what she will think and what, if any, sort of publisher would be interested. When I finally stop reading from my notes and look up at her, I notice a sliver of tears down her cheeks. She whispered, "My brother has schizophrenia, it's been hell both for my mother and I, please write the book."

On the Sunday morning, again, there is a general presentation by Dr Kim Etherington on "Writing first person stories for research". She is a psychotherapist, too, so my confidence is beginning to grow. Here, I am reintroduced to the concept of using "self" as a major tool in research. She puts up her slide:

> passionate and discerning involvement in problem solving: an effort to know the essence of some aspect of life through the internal pathways of the self. [Moustakas & Douglass, 1985, p. 39]

This is what I had been doing in my college assignments, using my experiences of the internal pathways of the self. I felt affirmed. I rushed to buy her book, too. I had much to learn.

I return home to London inspired by the events of the weekend. I read *The Wounded Storyteller* (Frank, 1995) and *Becoming a Reflexive Researcher: Using Ourselves in Research* (Etherington, 2004) as if they were the best thrillers in the world. I slowly came to realize that I was not a writer, but that it was equally valid to be the author of my own experiences. From this place, I resolved to write my publishing proposal. The seed of the book had germinated. It now had a tiny root and a small shoot bearing its first unfurled leaf.

Almost three years later. The seedling has flourished and grown falteringly into a little evergreen with small, green, glossy leaves. It is almost two feet high now but its main pale grey stem shows many gnarled scars where it has been pruned and cut back. It should flower, but it never has. I must have changed the type of compost it is in five or six times. I have had to patiently wait and watch it suffer from almost every plant disease you could think of. I thought plants were supposed to respond to human love and grow straight and true towards the light. At one point, I grew so concerned about it I used really quite strong pesticides and sprays on it, something I never normally do. Each spray developed other things wrong with it. It has had black spot, and white spot, and insect infestation. As it got over each disease, it seemed to develop another one. It seems so far to only flourish in the shade. I have tried putting it out in the bright sunshine, but its leaves just drooped within hours. Much of the time I have had to keep it away from other plants in case it passed on its myriad diseases.

It stands in an antique terracotta pot that has been weathered and worn by the elements for decades now. I like its faded battered look. I think for the first time there are some small flower buds starting to form. I hope they, too, don't develop some disease. I find it hard not to be pessimistic even though it is springtime. I wonder if now is the time to put it out in the light, and just trust in Nature that the inherent nature of the flower will find its own way of manifesting, or not.

At last, spring time has arrived, and now I can speculate on how the restitution, chaos, and quest narrative models of illness, developed by Frank (1995), might be applied to the illness and treatment of psychosis.

The *restitution narrative* of, "Yesterday I was healthy, today I am sick, but tomorrow I will be healthy again" has no place in the psychotic patients repertoire of stories. Not until after the patient has been "sick" does he even realize he has been ill. The restitution storyline always belongs to the medical narrative, not the personal narrative. In psychosis, according to the mental health professional, the narrative is, "Take the medication regularly and the chemical imbalance will be corrected". Restitution to full and functioning health does not come into the script.

Restitution stories reassure the listener that however bad things look, a happy ending is possible. In psychosis, as long as the psychiatric medication model is followed, a favourable outcome is presumed, even though it is generally acknowledged there are no cures. This is narrative surrender for the psychotic person and their families, who tacitly agree to tell their story in terms of psychiatric treatment. Nevertheless, the restitution narrative of psychosis, which can include a life-long sentence of psychiatric medication, is the one most commonly favoured in society as the only possible message of hope on offer.

However, the restitution narrative is now being challenged from within the psychiatric profession itself. Moncrieff (2007), in *The Myth of the Chemical Cure*, exposes as fraudulent the claims that psychiatric drugs correct chemical imbalances. Although psychiatrists talk of psychiatric drugs correcting a chemical imbalance there is, in fact, no proof that such an imbalance exists. Also, there is no concrete evidence for antipsychotic long-term effectiveness. Joanna Moncrieff is also a founder of the UK Critical Psychiatry Network, a group of psychiatrists who provide a critique of the current psychiatric system, and see drug use as having a minor role in the resolution of psychosis.

"The *chaos narrative* is the opposite of restitution: its plot imagines life never getting better" (Frank, 1995, p. 97). It feeds on the sense that no one is in control and promotes feelings of victimhood. In psychosis, the patient is not in control, the family is not in control, and psychiatry insists on maintaining its pretence of control through prescribing medication. The chaos story is also marked by the absence of a coherent voice; in psychosis the individual's ability to narrate their life as an evolving story in consensus reality is profoundly interrupted and diminished.

As the psychotic individual often cannot distinguish between consensus reality and altered states, their interrupted storyline is picked up and carried by family, friends, and mental health professionals. They then temporarily step into their wounded story and recognize their symptoms for them. They attempt to fill in the holes to create a sequential story. The wounded storyteller in psychosis invites and demands others into the storyline to help order their experience. As Frank movingly writes, "This suffering solicits me and calls me, eliciting in me a suffering for the suffering" (Frank, 1995, p. 177).

Psychosis is a many-layered story. Psychosis invokes feelings of disintegration, alienation, and isolation, marked by loss of contact with consensus reality, as well as a sense of social stigma. On top of that, the treatment sometimes involves force, and the side-effects of the medication are often difficult to tolerate. In the psychotic chaos narrative, "Troubles go all the way down to bottomless depths. What can be told only begins to suggest all that is wrong" (Frank, 1995, p. 99). The chaos narrative dominates the experience of psychosis, not just for the individual, but also for the family and friends, with its accompanying loss of voice. The chaos story itself can only be recounted outside the chaos and retrospectively.

It is only in the *quest narrative* that the teller has a story to tell. In the chaos story, the tale is too overwhelming, and in the restitution story, the tale is dictated by the mental health profession. In quest stories, "the quest is defined by the ill person's belief that something is to be gained through the experience" (Frank, 1995, p. 115). It is difficult, from a human individual viewpoint, to see that anything good can be gained from the experience of psychosis, such is the accompanying psychological suffering and excruciating pain. But quest stories also tell of searching for alternative ways of being ill. This is possibly one of the current narrative quests for psychosis. There can only be better ways of the illness being perceived by society. Society is suppressing the truth about the suffering around psychosis and its treatment and that truth must be told. There also needs to be an openness to more integrative forms of treatment and not just a blind acceptance of the psychiatric medication model as the only possible form of treatment.

I believe our challenge now is to tell our stories of psychosis. We need to fill in the gaps; tell the parts that have never been told. We need to honour the truth of how psychosis and its treatment affects individuals and their families. We need to tell our tales in all their messiness and complexity. We need to leave in the ragged edges and confront the shame that has stigmatized us into silence. For people to move their stories outside the professional viewpoint involves a profound assumption of personal responsibility, yet we have a responsibility not just to ourselves, but to guide others who will follow us.

At the same time, we have to recognize the uniqueness of the illness of psychosis and how it makes us aware of the power of the unconscious. We can no longer deny the existence of other realities, for delusions and hallucinations take us into other worlds, the dreaming world, the unconscious, and the collective unconscious. Simple narratives that focus only on consensus reality no longer hold true in the dense complexity of psychotic realities.

Paradoxically, the gift of psychosis has been one of the primary ways that psychiatrists and psychotherapists have come to understand how the human mind works. Earlier in the book, from my psychotherapy research, I introduced the concept that we are all the products of unconscious and uncontrollable forces in the mind. Psychosis provided Carl Jung with the prerequisite insights for his life-changing discovery of how the collective unconscious is present within us all. Jung developed a model of consciousness which involved two dynamic unconscious forces: the personal unconscious (which contains individual repressed or forgotten experiences, thoughts, and feelings), and the collective unconscious, which he theorized as a universal blueprint shared by all human beings.

According to Ellenberger (1970), when Jung was working with severe psychotic patients at the Burgholzi, he

> had been struck by the frequent occurrence of universal symbols (which he later called archetypes) in their delusions and hallucinations. This brought him to assume that there existed another realm of the unconscious, besides that of repressed representations, which was the object of Freud's inquiry. [Ellenberger, 1970, p. 670]

The collective unconscious is the aspect of the unconscious that manifests the "inherited" universal themes that run through all human life. It is the whole psychological history of the human race living on within us, the reservoir of our experiences as a species. The universal symbols (archetypes) occur in mythical narratives. If we think about our dreams, we often dream about images which are way outside our personal experience. Just recently, I had a dream that my mother's ceiling fell down. Out of the ceiling poured water and scores of armadillos. To my conscious knowledge, I have never seen nor thought about an armadillo. But maybe, through mythical narrative, I perceive life as an army of defended and armoured creatures, hopelessly out of control, in the sea of the unconscious. Somehow, my dream had tapped into the universal imagery of the collective unconscious of which I have no awareness.

Most religions have a tradition of dream interpretation. Dreams are an international and a universal language. The collective unconscious is a universal consciousness that holds the memories, experiences, and wisdom of the human race. Through dreams, we are connected to the collective unconscious, which unites us all beyond race, religion, or culture. The interconnectedness of all life is thus affirmed.

Myths are narratives that use these universal symbols to reveal a deeper underlying truth about what it means to be human. Joseph Campbell was the world's leading expert on comparative mythology. In his book, *Myths to Live By* (1973), he devotes a chapter to "Schizophrenia: the inward journey". He describes a psychotic breakdown as a condition where one has lost touch with the life and the thought of the community. He links the psychotic episode to the quest narrative. Very briefly, the usual pattern in the quest story is, first of all,

> ... a break away or departure from the local social order and context; next, a long, deep retreat inward and backward, backward, as it were, in time, and inward, deep into the psyche; a chaotic series of encounters there, darkly terrifying experiences, and presently (if the victim is fortunate) encounters of a centering kind, fulfilling, harmonizing, giving new courage; and then finally, in such fortunate cases, a return journey of rebirth to life. And that is the universal formula also of the mythological hero journey of separation, initiation, and return. [Campbell, 1973, p. 202]

Many eminent psychiatrists have also pointed out the similar themes found in myths and psychotic episodes, including Jung, Laing, and Perry. The relevance of myth to psychosis is explained by Campbell in the following way: that although the hero's journey is told in terms of princes and dragons, battles and ordeals, it is actually a metaphor for the venture into the psyche. Myth can be a very helpful metaphor in understanding the psychotic process. This leads to some of the alternative viewpoints that see psychosis as a spiritual crisis in which people break down to break through.

It is difficult, if not impossible, when the chaos narrative engulfs us, to give credence to the spiritual breakthrough that psychosis might offer. At the same time, I believe we have to honour the message that psychosis forces us to acknowledge the unconscious and hidden dimensions in our life and our need to respect the unfolding of unconscious archetypes and mythical dimensions. As family and friends, it is almost impossible to hear the mythical dimension when you are living in a chaos narrative. However, through professional ears, when we listen to psychotic stories, we can often hear the poetic echoes of our culture and its suffering; a story too unbearable to hold its coherence. When we are over-whelmed by the agonizing suffering involved in psychosis, we can barely function, but when we reflect later, we can also begin to glimpse the complexity and the unseen dimensions of the human mind, including the collective unconscious.

If we can tell and write our stories of psychosis, retrospectively and outside the fragmented and fractured chaos narrative, we create a possibility for change and a better future.

> In the telling of our stories we also learn what makes us similar, what connects us all, what helps us transcend the isolation that separates us from each other and from ourselves. [Remen, 2006, p. xxvii]

*   *   *

Postscript two

Two weeks exactly have passed since that first Saturday evening, when my friend unsuccessfully tried to have her son, Ken, sectioned. On the Monday, alerted by the crisis team, the regular Community Psychiatric Nurse (CPN) did a home visit to see Ken. He realized that Ken was losing the ability to look after himself by the state of his flat. However, he didn't think this warranted sectioning him. On that same Monday, my friend wrote to Ken's consultant psychiatrist asking for advice and help on out-of-hours sectioning.

The CPN requested the Home Treatment team to visit later in the week, in an attempt to try to get Ken to take the medication at home. When they called, there was no reply so they went away. Nothing else happened that week. On the Saturday, my friend rang her son and, for the first time that week, he picked up the phone. He seemed rational and said he was fine. She invited him to go out with her. When he turned up, he was smelly, in dirty old clothes, and laughing uncontrollably at nothing. She knew, however, his anger and aggression were barely concealed. That week, she had continued working, but each day she kept hoping to hear some news either from his psychiatrist or his mental health team. The fear of him being sectioned was huge, the fear of him not being sectioned was huge. When she knew the mental health teams could not get hold of him, this frightened her, too.

The following week the CPN went round again to find no reply. Midweek, the neighbours from Ken's block of flats made an official complaint to the Housing Association about the swarms of flies on the landing outside his flat. Swarms of flies are often associated with corpses. The Housing Association contacted the police and together they made a home visit. Again, there was no answer, so the police had to knock the door down. Ken was at home surrounded by flies. The police did a search, confiscated his cannabis, and left. The Housing Association officer took my friend's number from Ken, and rang her to ask if she could do something about the state of the flat. He also told her they were considering evicting Ken, which was another one of her nightmares.

Later that day, my friend went round, but could not enter without putting a scarf over her face because of the dense clouds of swarming flies. They were everywhere, on the ceiling, the floor, on the work surfaces. The stench of rotting rubbish was unbearable. She took out the garbage and sprayed the flies, using six large aerosol cans. She cleaned the brown sludge out of the sink and washed up the dirty dishes. Ken kept saying he was fine and there was nothing to worry about. He told her he was "Lord of the Flies", and the flies were just part of him thinking things out.

There was some small progress, for at last the Housing Association officer and the CPN were exchanging numbers and starting to work together. Now that the Housing Association was involved, the mental health team had a duty to protect the safety of the neighbours. That was a valid reason for them to section him: protecting the public. They arranged in two days' time to send a team in to section him; police, two doctors, the CPN, a social worker and the Housing Association officer.

My friend was still anxious about the sectioning. She knew Ken knew enough to be reasonable and how to work the system. He might be deeply psychotic, but he had his own methods of self-preservation. When he had been ill before, it was his standard practice not to open the door to anyone. She was terrified now that she had cleaned the flat that there would not be an immediate crisis. If the crisis management team did not see immediate danger they often did not do anything.

I asked her how many times Ken had been hospitalized. She is hugely intelligent and precise. She replied, "I have no idea. I have lost count, maybe three, four, five, or six times." She was clearly overwhelmed. I asked her whether maybe she should have tomorrow off work. She said she didn't want a day off; she did not want time to think. It was all too awful. She was left waiting in no man's land again, worried that he would be sectioned and worried that he wouldn't be. This wasn't stress; this was trauma.

It was Friday evening when my friend called. "They didn't section him today," she said. "They weren't able to get the full team together. They are trying again on Monday." She told me that she heard for the first time an apologetic tone in the CPN's voice; she realized that now he had to answer to the Housing Association as well.

She had also received a letter from Ken's psychiatrist. She read it out to me.

Thank you for your letter dated 01 March 2008.

I am sorry to learn the difficulties/frustration you faced while trying to get Ken assessed by the out-of-hours emergency social worker. In your letter you wanted guidance from me how to deal with a crisis during out-of-hours. I want to clarify that out-of-hours emergency social services department acts independently and we (mental health services) do not have any influence on this service. In case of a crisis, your option could be either to call the police if you feel unsafe and intimidated by Ken or persuade him to go the to A&E at the Hospital where they have a Mental Health Liaison Service.

In an acute emergency you could ask the on-call GP to help you to assess him if you feel he is not willing to attend A&E.

Consultant Psychiatrist

She told me she was stunned by the psychiatrist's lack of interest in Ken, although he had been a patient of hers for three years. I asked her how she was feeling. She replied, "I daren't stop and pause for even a minute. I am in that jittery nervy state and I have another weekend of non-stop worry about what he might do." I heard her drag on her cigarette: the cigarettes she so successfully gave up last year when she had a heart scare.

CHAPTER SEVEN

The power of the
multi-generational psyche

Diary extract

Eighteen months have now passed since I last wrote in my journal. Time has simply disappeared into the spaces between the long-term project of my son's aftercare recovery programme and the short-term, difficult, one-way-ticket project of looking after my mother's deteriorating dementia and her inexorable march towards death itself. In the hours in between, I had continued working as a therapist, and also embarked on some new training as a systemic constellation therapist.

I had been suffering, for most of this time, a severe case of "theomania". This was a word coined by Scott Peck, to describe "the illusion that we can be the scriptwriter in the drama of our lives" (Peck, 1993, p. 193). During this period, I was running and funding, single-handed, one private mental health hospital for depression and dementia, and an integrative aftercare recovery programme for psychosis, at different ends of the country. There seemed to be no respite from my storyline of living with mental illnesses. My general fatigue meant I became increasingly resentful of my script; worse than that, I found myself becoming frustrated and downright angry with the scriptwriter(s). Where had all my training gone? I remembered my carefully thought through definition of the transpersonal in the foreword: "the transpersonal approach seeks to acknowledge, yet move beyond, the awareness of the individual 'self' as a separate, isolated consciousness. It seeks to embrace a more interrelated, universal, complex sense of being which is in harmony with an unseen order of things and recognizes there exists beyond ourselves a powerful force that nurtures our growth and evolution".

Even though I had written that, I was finding it difficult to hold any perspective beyond the misery of my individual "self", through witnessing the suffering of my son and mother and what felt like the curse of mental illness. To put it mildly, I was not getting on with upstairs at all. I wished they would get a new bunch of scriptwriters. I didn't feel nurtured by my experiences, nor could I sense a powerful force interested in my growth and evolution. As for harmony with an unseen order of things, my experience was of discord and exhaustion. In fact, if I had had a punch bag, it would probably be beaten into soft pulp by now, except I didn't have enough energy for that either.

I felt that I had accompanied Scott Peck through all his books on "the road less travelled", and "further along the road less travelled". I was now on "the road less travelled and beyond" and there seemed to be very few signs of the route turning into anything other than sheer slog and suffering. The only welcoming café I came across was my new-found training programme in constellation work. I also drew support from my fellow travellers from the original weekend workshop, but, apart from that, it was one long lonely trip, despite the fact that I was busy dealing with mental health professionals one way or another, day in and day out.

My main priority, of course, was still my son, even though we were now in the period referred to as aftercare. Any symptoms of psychosis had long since disappeared, but although we had moved out of the darkness it seemed difficult to disperse the accompanying shadows.

My son's aftercare package was designed to be integrative, but we, of course, had no precedent to follow. It was fraught, long, and difficult. After a year, he had been discharged by the psychiatrist as being in remission. He remained still on an eighth of a tablet of the

lowest dose of his medication. He continued with the orthomolecular treatment, but now saw a nutritionist who was also a kiniesi-
ologist. Her method of treatment was to muscle test his body for
which supplements were supporting his unique bodily responses to
the drugs, etc. He continued with his Tai Chi and his process orientated therapy.

Although my son had gone through the day centre and the
cognitive–behaviour therapy and had gradually reduced his drugs,
profound fatigue and generalized anxiety were still apparent. This
time, of course, was different, because my son was actively
involved in his own treatment plan and was personally committed
to regaining his health. What was the hardest thing to manage was
the nervous apprehension of the illness returning. No one yet had
invented any medicine or psychotherapeutic approach that would
take away the fear that the unwanted, shameful, bullying guest
might return.

The information I found on aftercare programmes was very
different from the causal theories I had previously read. Suddenly,
it seemed that parental and familial influence was recognized by
the mental health professionals as having a profound influence on
the illness.

> The emphasis is no longer on the family as a source of pathology,
> but as a major instrument of restoration to health. [Arieti, 1981,
> p. 136]

> The right parenting can do more for schizophrenics than the right
> drugs. [James, 2004]

> However, research has revealed an important role the family can
> play in helping in the recovery of a person with psychotic experi-
> ences. In particular, attitudes of friends and relatives towards the
> person, and how they understand and react to the person's experi-
> ences are very important. They can also influence the extent to
> which the person is able to recover. [Mental Health Care, 2008]

In the mental health profession, the evidence is robust that the way
families react has a powerful impact on the course of the illness. As
a result, we are given guidelines on how to help our loved ones.
These strategies include managing our family interactions and not

using "high expressed emotion" with our relatives. This describes our potential critical or hostile behaviour, or being overly protective or over-involved, which encourages their dependence; either of these responses maybe seen as a possible cause of relapse in their recovery.

As families, we are indirectly judged for our possible critical behaviour. At the same time, we are excluded from the treatment plan through rendering us voiceless and thereby infantilizing us.

These guidelines on "high expressed emotion" are, of course, helpful as markers for us to try to avoid. Criticism, in any event, is a demeaning experience, and is essentially fault-finding. The tone of voice and the intention behind remarks are more important than their content. It is possible, for instance to tell someone to "F off" as an expression of endearment; if it is said in playful mode, with a warm smile, it can act as a mild rebuke but with a loving heart. When I first started my training as a psychotherapist, I wondered how I would fare putting myself in the firing line for constant feedback in my weekly therapy and throughout the group training. I was so highly attuned to the critical content of my mother's voice, I was used to hearing criticism when there wasn't any. Learning about genuine feedback on how someone is doing, both when they are doing well and when they are not, is essentially built on a matter of trust: I know this person has my well being at heart, therefore I can listen even though I may hear how my behaviour is not being well received.

Trust is an essential element in recovery from psychosis, as alienation and isolation are its predominating symptoms. Building trust so that the patient knows the family are behind them and wanting their recovery then becomes the primary goal. Building trust between the families, patients, and mental health professionals could then become the secondary goal.

From my own experience it is, at times, virtually impossible not to feel critical and hugely angry with someone in an altered state of consciousness when they are uttering the thoughts of the unwelcome bullying guest with unswayable convictions that they and they alone are right. In my weekend workshop, it was the common shared experience of human fallibility without the fear of being criticized that led the participants to be able to admit their own mistakes and blind spots. This, in turn, made it possible for them to experience some lightening of their huge burdens of guilt, shame, and isolation. As in other successful self-support groups, such as Al Anon, for the families of alcoholics, it is not the medical profession that eases their emotional pain: it is through sharing their experiences that they gain strength to find their own ways forward. Peer support groups for the family and friends of sufferers of psychosis could best find their own ways forward through sharing the enormous challenges in dealing with altered states of consciousness.

However, within the medical profession, the involvement of family and friends is generally only deemed important when the patient is transferred to the aftercare programme. At this juncture, the mental health profession does an about turn and emphasizes their importance in preventing relapse. This is in direct contrast to the pain of enforced non-involvement families and carers experience during the earlier stages of treatment. All the pain is eloquently expressed in two emails I recently received:

> In a nutshell—my son (please don't mention him by name) started to become ill when he was around seventeen (twelve years ago), which we put down to teenage behaviour. After many stressful years he was eventually sectioned and put into a secure hospital that took me four months and many tribunals to get him released from. The hospital was like something out of *One Flew Over the Cuckoo's Nest* and has had long-lasting psychological damage on my son. The hospital is now under investigation. Many years on and no marked improvement later, he is in yet another place and we are currently trying to arrange the all important, but ever scarce, after care. This is the time when many people with psychosis decide they are better and come off the medication. The all too common pattern of Step 1: hospitalisation + medication; Step 2: Return home + medication; Step 3: feel better +stop medication; Step 4: Stop medication + relapse; Step 1: hospitalisation + medication. This whole repetitive cycle is an exhausting, emotional nightmare.

> Stephan won't go to see the CPN (Psychiatric Nurse, NHS) I arranged and then the dichotomy is that they won't make an effort to see him if he won't make the effort himself. I can't act on his behalf without his consent. DON'T THEY REALISE THEY HAVE CONDITIONS THAT RENDER THEM IRRATIONAL!!!!! I've said this to so many doctors and nurses about me acting on his behalf. It's SUCH hard thankless work. I'm currently looking in to

supported housing but I can't arrange anything without him making an effort, which he won't and often goes missing when I try to pin him down. I have the unenviable position of trying to again get him to the CPN tomorrow. Who knows??????

The problem of the patient not continuing the medication once they believe they no longer need it is an all too familiar one. In fact, the efficacy of psychiatric medication is not measured in the reduction of the symptoms, but the length of time the patient will take it for. This, of course, is directly related to the many unpleasant side effects of the antipsychotic drugs. Once again, the parents and primary carers often carry the symptoms of knowing when their relative is not taking the medication. Recently, a client told me that when her son stopped taking the medication, the CPN stopped going round as he was not complying with their treatment plan. It was a ludicrous and no-win situation. The patients that have access to outreach teams who continue to monitor the medication seem to fare best.

Although the benefits of counselling and support for the family are recognized by the Department of Health and the National Institute for Clinical Excellence (NICE), particularly in relation to the prevention of relapses, unfortunately, this approach has yet to be incorporated into general service provision. An integrated after-care package that includes the voices and experiences of the patient, primary carers, and outreach mental health teams would, I believe prove to be more effective than the current fragmented system.

Seemingly unable to escape the world of mental health problems, I now had to deal with my mother's depression and dementia. The combination of being an only child and my mother's self-imposed isolated lifestyle meant this fell entirely on my shoulders. For the first few months of her diagnosis, when she did not recognize the symptoms herself, I could do very little. She had been as good as her word and had instructed her GP and the Elderly Mentally Ill unit not to release any information to me. I wrote to them explaining my position and categorically saying I was there should I be needed. Our secret tortuous relationship was now out in the open for all to see.

She had already been prescribed Aricept and some vitamins, but at this stage she was not on antidepressants. She had a weekly visit from the Mental Health Team. I set up a private nursing agency to go round once a day to check she had taken the tablets. Very often she would not let them in. Eventually the agency rang and told me she had instructed them not to return. When I rang, she either complained about her isolation or refused to speak to me. Christmas was almost here, and my son was still in early recovery mode and wanted to stay in London. As a compromise, I wrote and said that I would go up the day after Boxing Day and stay for a few days. On Christmas morning, my son handed me the phone and said, "It is Gran." She said she did not want my visit as she didn't want her house sullied with my presence. I spent Christmas morning in tears. Even with all my years of training, sometimes it was impossible for me not to take the symptoms of her depression personally. On an unconscious level, she was making sure I felt like she did. That is how it works. On that Christmas morning she transferred her feelings on to me and I was left carrying her depression.

In the New Year I wrote to her, asking if we could mend the bridge of silence between us, but she didn't reply. On Mother's Day, like the dutiful daughter I was, I sent flowers. She telephoned immediately and was sweetness and light, waxing lyrical about the gorgeous lilies. That was when I realized that her memory really was going. But at last I was back in the picture.

At the onset of her illness, the GP and I had arranged for my mother to make a regular weekly visit to the village practice. So I was careful to co-ordinate my next visit to incorporate this. When I arrived, I noted that the garden was still immaculate, but the house was beginning to mirror her inner state of confusion: papers and flyers littered most surfaces, together with her written notes and lists. She lucidly told me within minutes that she was losing her mind. She reminded me that it was Tuesday and she had a doctor's appointment that afternoon. I insisted on going with her for the walk through the village; very reluctantly, she agreed.

In the waiting room, in front of other patients and the receptionist, we had a hugely embarrassing row when she insisted that she did not want me to go in to see the doctor with her. But I had an agenda and nothing was going to stop me. I registered the look of surprise on the doctor's face when he saw me. I imagined he thought I was the world's worst daughter. The beginning of the consultation was strictly between them. After a few minutes, I told the doctor that the illness was getting my mother down and that she was crying each day. The fact was, my mother had been crying every day for the last thirty years. The doctor asked her if it was true. She nodded silently in agreement. He asked her if she would like some tablets to help. I heard her say, "Yes, please." I knew she didn't really understand that she was being offered antidepressants, but I was desperate for some tablet, any tablet, with any side-effects, that would help both her and me through the downright misery of her symptoms of depression.

The doctor referred her on to a gerontology psychiatrist. She had recently had a brain scan because of her fear that she had developed a brain tumour. I, of course, accompanied her. The psychiatrist said the scan showed only minor shrinkage. He asked my mother about the circumstances of her life. She told him that she was getting over a failed love affair, that she was very isolated, and needed to move house. I was not included in the session. An invisible elastoplast had been firmly placed over my mouth. The failed love affair was a fantasy based on a very small incident. There had never been a relationship; it existed solely in her mind as a means of escape from the grim reality of her lonely life. She had been wanting to move house for sixteen years now. I was amazed that the psychiatrist took what she said at face value without seeking any contextual information from me. How many more times would I have to go on having this experience?

Another Christmas came and went. The tablets had made her so much more affable and reasonable. We all went to stay with her. She did not really know it was Christmas, even though I had decorated the house. I am back into "normalizing" with Christmas trees and turkey and all the trimmings. I have lost my centre yet again.

With my fortnightly visits now routine, I never failed to see a marked deterioration. Yet, she was happier than I had ever known her. She now looked forward to my visits. What was absolutely extraordinary was how she kept going. The evidence of the power of automatic unconscious behaviour was re-enforced within me. She was existing on automatic pilot. The familiar routines of her home just kept her going right down to her habitual completion of the codeword and crossword. It seemed to me that it was the visual clues that gave her life meaning. She did everything she had always done, except she did not go out of the village unaccompanied.

One day, as part of our new routine, I drove her to the large Sainsbury's to do the weekly shopping. She took the trolley and ran a few steps, and then started sliding down the aisle, giggling. After a while, the socially conformist part of me pointed out that nobody else was sliding down the aisle. "Oh don't worry darling," she says, "it will soon catch on."

At the end of the dark winter months, I became very alarmed by her weight loss of a stone in three weeks. She was very thin and frail now. The doctor, too, was concerned. He told me gravely that there might be cancer involved as well. He suggested that she go into hospital and have a series of tests. Because a physical illness was suspected, she could claim on her health insurance. She had no awareness of what was really happening. She kept saying, "If I am in hospital that must mean I should be worried." Her dementia was kind, because she could not keep consistent and consecutive thought patterns, and could not remember to be anxious. The nursing home was monitoring her food intake. It turned out that she ate absolutely everything. After three days of tests, I had an appointment with the consultant. He came into the waiting room and sat beside me. He had a warm, concerned face and a lovely, reassuring consultant's voice. He told me that they could find nothing else wrong apart from the obvious vascular deterioration. My face could not hide the fact that I was bewildered by the news. I had been preparing myself for something very different. I said falteringly, "I find that difficult, I don't know what to do now." He nodded, and put his hand on my arm and said, "You are doing all the worrying for her. You are carrying all the symptoms. That is a very hard thing to have to do."

As if by magic, my heavy, polished steel suit of armour and visor simply dissolved into thin air, revealing at last my crumpled, fragile, hurting self. My part in the illness had been named. I had been seen and understood. Travelling back to London on the all too familiar train, I somehow felt lighter. The insight into how I had been carrying the symptoms of my son's illness, my mother's lifelong battle with depression, and now her dementia, even helped dissolve some of the density of my silver-grey mantle. The train rattled and rolled along the track, clickety click, clickety click, clickety click. And then it came to me, psychosis in the family means, families carry the symptoms, families carry the symptoms, families carry the symptoms.

Halfway back to London, my thoughts turned back to my son. What I really wanted to find was a glossy brochure or swish website for a smart new Integrative Psychiatric Day Clinic. In their absence, I created it solely in my mind.

The Integrative Psychiatry Day Clinic

"What is useful, what helps, what heals?" (Bert Hellinger)

Our Integrative Psychiatry Day Clinic offers a new developmental programme adopting a combined holistic and orthodox approach to psychosis. We aspire to use collective intelligence to promote the well being of mind, body, and spirit.

We welcome patients and their families (and primary carers), and offer respect to all practitioners. We embrace an appreciation of differences and necessary opposition and an awareness of fundamental commonalities.

We provide aftercare recovery programmes for mild to moderate psychological distress, as well as access to a network of early intervention outreach services. Our programme is designed to offer comprehensive integrative care packages to both sufferers and their families and carers.

Individual integrative treatment plans are devised and managed by teams consisting of the patient, primary carers, psychiatrist, psychotherapist, and other complementary therapists. Treatment plans aim to address the symptoms as well as root causes of psychosis. We utilize conventional medication where necessary, but enhance this through holistically supported medication reduction plans for gradual detoxification. Orthomolecular medicine is used as standard practice in optimizing health and reducing the toxic effects of drug treatment. Our in-house dispensary stocks conventional medicines together with a wide range of vitamins, minerals, amino acids, enzymes, and essential fatty acids.

You will be welcomed into our calm and peaceful clinic by knowledgeable reception staff who are able to introduce you to all our facilities, including the newly formed Integrative Psychiatry Department. Many of our clinic staff are recovering patients or their family members, and our highly experienced professional practitioners come from a wide range of disciplines who have specialized in psychosis.

A variety of complementary therapies, which have proved effective in alleviating the distress of psychosis, are available including:

- Autogenic Therapy
- Narrative Therapy, Writing Workshops, Understanding Spiritual Narratives
- Ecological Medicine
- Systemic Constellation Therapy
- Human Givens Therapy
- Acupuncture
- Massage

We also offer:

- Individual psychotherapy and counselling services. Mentoring.
- Regular facilitated support groups for patients' families, friends, and siblings. We also support the growth of self-help groups nationally.
- Encouragement to patients to form their own societies such as the recent highly successful initiative, "Hearing Voices".
- Organic cafe serving a range of nutritionally balanced, gluten free and dairy free meals.
- Library and bookshop stocking a wide range of books on mental health and psychiatry, including a section written by sufferers themselves, with regular discussion groups providing the opportunity to hear from authors.
- Guest lectures and conferences including the annual International Conference on Integrative and Holistic Medicine for Aftercare programmes of Psychosis.

Additionally, our press office works hard to educate the media to understand that psychosis is a blameless illness, just like any other illness. We hope to influence future reporting to recognize psychosis as involving mild, moderate, severe, or enduring psychological distress. We fully support *the Campaign to Abolish Schizophrenia Labelling.*

I fantasized that Prince Charles would be the clinic's patron, and celebrity status would follow for the very first time as people "came out" and owned psychosis in their own family without fear of stigma or shame.

The idealist in me dreams of such a place, but the realist wonders where the funding would come from.

*   *   *

Postscript three

At last, on the following Monday, Ken was sectioned. My friend was surprised that he hadn't agreed to go voluntarily: one of his mottos was "Never get sectioned. Always go voluntarily".

That evening she visited Ken in the brand spanking new mental health unit. He was still aggressive and angry. He shouted abuse and used his size to intimidate the male Staff Nurse, who wouldn't give him a lighter. The following day was the usual ward round with the Consultant, the Registrar, the CPN, the student doctor, the trainee social worker, the Occupational Therapist, the Ward Manager, and the Staff Nurse. My friend and her son joined them. On hearing the usual "How are you feeling Ken?" he immediately burst into another tirade of abuse about being sectioned: "Don't you know you can't section someone just because their flat is a mess!!??" "Thank you Ken," said the consultant, politely dismissing him. "We must get him on medication before he hurts someone," he announced. My friend thought miserably that that was what she had been saying for several weeks now.

Over the four weeks that Ken was in hospital, he continued to improve, although at times he was severely over-medicated. My friend and Ken's father used the time to refurbish his flat, which my friend described as surprisingly therapeutic. At last they felt involved and that they could do something to help.

Ken's new treatment plan, for the first time in his long history, included a referral for cognitive–behavioural therapy; he was no longer on depot injections, which he found humiliating, and was put on oral medication. Unfortunately, his next appointment with the psychiatrist was still a long six weeks away.

My friend was now back in the all too common pattern of after-care: step 1: hospitalization + medication leading to feeling better and stopping the medication, etc. Just right now, she prefers to believe in the triumph of hope over experience.

My friend felt considerable relief when they "put away" her son after his potentially aggressive behaviour. Because she was at her wits' end she even welcomed the sledgehammer approach of sectioning. She had been pressed to the limits of her emotional and mental resources. In this pathetically grateful place, she welcomed psychiatric services with open arms, and lost sight of the mental health services failure to act both promptly and compassionately. Ken should not have had to experience being Lord of the Flies.

Reflections on the power of the multi-generational psyche

Now that I am almost a year into the aftercare programme, I notice at last that the chaos narrative that things would never get better is beginning to recede. Throughout, I have used my autogenic therapy practice to help me deal with my internal stress responses. Only now, as I come out of the chaos, do I begin to realize that I have been more than just in fight or flight mode.

In the fractured and fragmented story of living with someone with psychosis, the effects of trauma reign. Anxiety, hopelessness, and confusion are the order of the day, together with an unerring belief that these feelings will never end. The trauma–emergency response is characterized by freezing or fragmenting, experienced as a dulling of the senses, combined with keeping busy with distracting behaviour patterns (Ruppert, 2008, p. 58). Quiet reflective periods are avoided as being too painful. Just as in the post-script, my friend could not take a day off work when her son Ken was ill, I too, have just blindly kept on going, keeping myself busy all the way through.

It is important to realize that there are two types of trauma. The first type of trauma is, of course, the more widely recognized model of brief, sudden, and unexpected events, characterized by acute danger to life and limb, e.g., accidents, rape, natural catastrophes. I was responding to the second type of trauma, as a witness to trauma in the form of persistent and repetitive situations that overwhelmed me and left me feeling helpless and powerless (*ibid.*, p. 56) At last I can understand my own experiences better when I realize that witnesses of trauma are also traumatized.

Trauma does not just affect the physical body. It also has an impact on the mind, soul, and ability to interrelate socially. Other general consequences include hyper-vigilance, extreme anxiety, and feelings of helplessness and hopelessness. I definitely experienced all of these, as well as manifesting another typical response to trauma: the capacity to normalize that which is not normal. In retrospect, it is reassuring to know that, in my own crazy way, I had been behaving "normally" when faced with the trauma of witnessing unpredictable and seemingly illogical altered states of consciousness.

Because of my scattered thinking in the chaos period, there were some avenues of research I had not followed up. At the height of my son's illness, I had found a website, systemicfamilysolutions. com, about the philosopher and psychotherapist, Bert Hellinger, which stated, "Schizophrenia is not personal—it affects the whole family. You need only work with a member of the family, not the schizophrenic person. The main influence comes from those who were excluded." I had no idea what "the main influence comes from those who were excluded" meant, but at last I had found someone who shared my viewpoint that psychosis affects the whole family. That, combined with the idea that I could possibly help my son without him even being there, presented an irresistible avenue of exploration.

I had heard only passing reference to Bert Hellinger during my training, but I soon discovered that he is probably one of Europe's most innovative and provocative psychotherapists. Hellinger introduced the idea of transgenerational theories into the world of psychotherapy through identifying that there are certain loyalties and fates in the family that are transmitted down through the generations through the operation of unconscious family consciences. He also developed family or systemic constellation therapy as a pioneering method of disentangling current members of a family from the unresolved issues of previous generations.

While trawling through the Internet in search of information about systemic constellation therapy, I came across the work of Professor Franz Ruppert and his paper "Psychosis and schizophrenia:

disturbed bonding in the family system" (Ruppert, 2002). I only skim read it, but knew I wanted to follow it up. However, as he worked in Munich, I simply filed the information away for another day.

Now I was well into the aftercare phase, my perceptions were starting to sharpen up again. Even though I felt like a rag doll running up and down the country with my "carer's" hat on, I was just beginning to reflect back on the chaotic days of my son's illness without feeling totally overwhelmed. Inspired by the writing week- end workshop, I had even begun to put some thoughts down on paper for my publishing proposal. But, even though my life was so busy, some unseen hand made me once again turn on the computer to look up Franz Ruppert's work. I could not believe it; he was coming to do a workshop in Bristol in three weeks' time in July. I decided to book it immediately. I had absolutely no idea that this was, in fact, his very first teaching seminar in England.

On the train to Bristol, I reread the description of the workshop:

July 2005

TRAUMA, BONDING and FAMILY CONSTELLATIONS

New Perspectives on Mental Illnesses and Its Treatment
with Professor Franz Ruppert

"How is it that some people lose their mental stability for no obvi- ous reason that can be found in their life experience?

"It is suggested that the family constellation approach offers a way of clarifying the hidden dynamics in families that may result in the symptoms of mental illnesses".

Professor Franz Ruppert: Franz has been Professor of Psychology at the University of Applied Sciences, Munich since 1992. He has writ- ten several books in German on this subject.

Constellations Work Trainings

When I considered that people might lose their mental stability without an obvious reason in their own life experience, it made me think about my son. To all intents and purposes, I had not been able to discern any specific events that could be seen as a precipitating factor to cause a breakdown of the psyche.

On the train to Bristol, I fantasized about writing the book. When I had done this three-day course and read some of Franz's papers, I could include his theories in the book and perhaps devote a chapter to them. Definition of arrogance: conceit, haughtiness, egotism. All this combined with yet another attack of "theomania" that I could be the scriptwriter of my own life.

I arrive at Oddfellows Hall and enter the large circle of chairs. There were about thirty participants there, most of them experienced constellation therapists. I do not know anyone and I do not know what I am about to experience. For three days I watch people take their current problems to Franz and then, under his direction, set up representatives for their family members in a constellation. I watch live enactments of people's family systems, showing their previously hidden traumas of war, betrayal, abuse, secrets, and untimely deaths. I am a silent witness to watching evidence of the deeply encoded affects of these traumatic events on future generations. I watch the inherent grief and unspoken memories etched on the faces of those who followed the traumatized ones. I notice that, as they acknowledge the past events, their faces seem lighter, as if some burden has been invisibly lifted.

One evening, Franz gives a slide show on his theories. The first slide says

"What is a 'psycho-trauma'?"

Psychological trauma: I don't get it. I have never experienced a trauma; I am a baby-boomer, a post-war girl from a war-free generation. My mother has depression, that's all.

On the train going home, I reflect on the weekend. I could not do a constellation because I was the last participant to sign up and there was no time. I had not been chosen once in three days to be a representative for anyone's family member. I realized, a little uncomfortably, that I was the only person in the room not to have participated once. I consider doing the constellation training, but the voice in my head tells I am all trained up as a coach, psychotherapist, and autogenic therapist. I have too much on my plate, including a book to write.

However, when I return home my experiences of the weekend stay with me; not the vivid tragedies enacted in the family constellations, but my own experience of having been the only person in the room who did not participate. In three days, in constellations involving often large numbers of people, this was against all the odds. Fortunately, I had done enough group work in my training to know that this was not a normal phenomenon for me. I decided I needed to do just one constellation of my own for the experience. When I surf the Internet, I find there is a constellation weekend in three weeks' time round the corner from where I live. When I sign up, it is confirmed that everyone will get to do their own piece of work. I notice how synchronistically things seemed to be happening.

I turn up to find just ten participants there. The first morning, two people set up their family groups with representatives from the circle. I am the only person not chosen to work in either. In the last constellation, all of the other nine people are in the constellation. I go home for lunch. I start shaking and cannot understand what is happening. When I go back I am determined to work with these feelings. My usual behaviour pattern of waiting until last in the group is jettisoned. My emotional state is guiding me. When the facilitator asks who wants to work, I cannot put my hand up quickly enough. When he asks me what I want to work with, I tell him about my overwhelming experience of feeling invisible and not included in the group that morning. The facilitator asks me to set up my family of origin. I choose representatives for my mother and father and my maternal grandparents.

When I see the representative of my father, I cannot stop shaking and I start to weep uncontrollably. He has been invisible to me my whole life. My mother left him when I was five and I had never seen or heard from him since. I was never even allowed to mention him. He had been totally excluded from the family system. He might have been shut out of my conscious mind, but when I see his representative, the power of the bond between us is undeniable.

The facilitator shows me that although I had been disconnected from him in life and he had been invisible, I had stayed deeply connected to him through my feelings of invisibility and exclusion. Out of my love for him I had remained like him. Now that I had seen him in the constellation meant that I, too, could be seen.

Slowly, I began to realize how, all my life, my senses had been deadened towards him. It was as if I did not have any feelings for him. I had simply normalized it. It was fine not to know who your father was. I realize how strong his unconscious influence had been on my life. I think of Bert Hellinger's words on that first website, "the main influence comes from those who have been excluded". The only thing I thought I had that belonged to him was a copy of his death certificate I had found three years earlier; now I realized that some of my inner feelings of being invisible and excluded also might belong to him. Just as the consultant had pointed out that I was carrying the symptoms of my mother's dementia, which she was unable to do for herself, I was unconsciously carrying my father's feelings too.

Two weeks after doing the constellation, I am on my way back from Yorkshire when I receive a telephone call from my mother's cousin. As an adult, I have only ever seen her three or four times at weddings and funerals. She has always remained in telephone contact with my mother, as they grew up on the same street and had always been friends. She tells me she realizes that my mother's memory is going. I confirm she has dementia, and explain how I am doing my best but that my mother's depression often prevents me from helping her. She acknowledges my mother's depression, too. She tells me she, too, is trained as a counsellor. It is good to talk to someone in the family honestly about my mother; it is a new experience for me.

But then she tells me something else.

"I've been wanting to ring you for years now to tell you how much I liked your father. He was intelligent and witty. I think it was wrong that you weren't allowed to see him; that you grew up without knowing him. Your mother always painted a totally black version of him, but I always liked and admired him. You need to know, he did want to remain in contact with you, but your grandfather and mother forbade it."

I am stunned. I feel a strong bond with her and instinctively trust her. She is, of course, from Yorkshire, and tells it as it is. Then she says, "I hope you don't think I am barmy, but I feel as if your father has been prompting me to make this phone call."

All these years of enforced silence and secrets, and now I have done the constellation it is as if something has been released in my family soul. I do not yet know that "Through systemic family theory, any changes in the person participating will also affect the family field. But because it's an interactive process, the family field will, in turn, affect the person" (Sheldrake & Beaumont, 2002, p. 58). I remember Franz's flyer for the workshop: *Trauma, Bonding and Family Constellations*. I realize that I have been traumatized since the age of five by not knowing the identity of my father, with whom I am deeply bonded. I had no photographs, no memorabilia, but worse than that was having had to wear that damn invisible elastoplast over my mouth all these years.

I look on the web for Systemic Constellation Therapy Training. A training starts in two weeks time. Skates on, I sign up; no matter I have my mother and son to look after.

On the first day we meet our trainer, Dr Albrecht Mahr. He introduces himself as a qualified doctor, trained in psychiatry, who has completed a ten-year psychoanalytic training. He also tells us that he was chair of the International Bert Hellinger Association, 1999–2004.

During the first seminar, I learn that family constellation work is not a therapy, but a philosophy based on the concept of natural systemic laws: a philosophy which invites us to move beyond our narrow view of individualism towards a wider sense of ourselves as part of larger systems; the first one being our immediate family. I learn that everyone is an integral part of the relationship systems in which he or she lives and everyone has an equal value in the functioning of those systems. As Hellinger so eloquently points out, "Every*one* in the family system is essential to the system" (Hellinger, Weber, & Beaumont, 1998, p. 70). This is the natural systemic law, that no one can be excluded and everyone has an equal right to belong, whatever their past actions.

Over the next two years, I do the training, continue studying with Franz, and go to Washington to see Bert Hellinger. It is an extraordinary time of personal discoveries.

I trace my half-brother from my father's second marriage. From him, at last, I find out about my father's life. When he was eighteen, he joined the Air Force and became a navigator in the Second World War. He was chosen for the Dam Busters, but never flew with them. After his five-year marriage to my mother, he remarried and had two sons. He worked as a Housemaster at a public school, but had a breakdown in his early forties. He suffered from post traumatic stress disorder through being unable to make any plans whatsoever for the future. He died on his sixtieth birthday of a heart attack.

I was acknowledged by the members of his second family; they even had early photographs of me. Every year they remembered my birthday. He paid private detectives to try to find me, but was unsuccessful, presumably because my mother had changed my name. On one occasion, my brother remembered him being very excited and telling him, they think they have found her. For half a century I had gone on believing he had no interest in me, but even that erroneous belief could not break the deep unconscious and yet alive emotional bond that continues to exist between us, even though he is dead.

Through my direct experience, I have come to understand Franz's theories that bonds are unconscious, but active living relationship systems that relate individuals and their families. Bonding starts at conception and keeps us all interrelated through the active force of love. Bonding also connects us beyond the family, and connects people who share common feelings, ideas, and activities.

Now, when I see any references to the Second World War, I feel for my father as a tall, skinny, eighteen-year-old youth, climbing into his plane with his heart in his mouth, as he set off on those night raids. What must his thoughts have been: would he be back for breakfast or would he be shot to pieces?

As Ruppert writes,

> That the human psyche can be traumatised and injured just as the human body can is not a completely new insight, but it has taken a long time for the idea to be widely accepted, and even now is still not well enough recognised in most of the societies . . . The infliction of psychological and emotional hurt on others is so common that most of us do not want to see what is really going on. If we did, we would then have to acknowledge that war, for example, which quite deliberately produces death and physical wounding, also causes psychological and emotional injury to the survivors, including those who may not have been physically injured. [Ruppert, 2008, p. 54]

Because we are all embedded in a complex system of bonding relationships over three or four generations, emotional problems and traumas are passed on from one generation to the next. Not only that, but when acute psychological trauma is experienced by an individual, some of the unbearable feelings are sometimes shared or shifted and taken over by others in the family in an unconscious attempt to alleviate the individual's pain.

Although not using the same vocabulary of the importance of bonding relationships, there seems to be a new understanding emerging of the impact of our relationships and social context on our psychological well being in other disciplines besides systemic constellation work.

Bentall (2003), in *Madness Explained*, describes the mind–brain as ". . . a biologically evolved but flexible cognitive system, which adapts to its environment by learning from other mind–brains (notably its caregivers)" (p. 202). He also notes that ". . . psychiatric theories that consider the brain in isolation from the social world are unlikely to lead us to a proper understanding of the origins of psychosis" (pp. 202–203).

There are also new developments in the understanding of genetic inheritance as a social phenomena. In the past, we have understood genetic inheritance as something fixed and encoded within our being, but this is now being questioned as an over-simplistic and incomplete idea based on genetic determinism. Rossi (2002) believes that these theories need to be amended

> ". . . to include the complementary concept that human experience can modulate gene expression. . . . The science of psychosocial genomics explores how creative human experience modulates gene expression as well as vice versa" (p. 15).

Paul Broks, the neuropsychologist, concurs with Rossi in his realization that ". . . the mind [is] the product of the brain in its interaction with the physical and social world" (2003, p. 60).

Ruppert's theories on psychosis also resonate with these latest findings. He clearly states that although trauma may be experienced as a psychological symptom, trauma is always related to larger social events, even if they occurred generations back. He also takes the view that the mind is a multi-generational phenomenon, and that psychotic patients are only symptom bearers for the systemic trauma.

Following on from these observations he writes,

> The acceptance of the notion that a patient's psychological conflict may not originate from their own experiences, but might indeed be

inherited from their ancestors would fundamentally change our view and practice of psychotherapy. It would amount to a revolution in the different schools of psychiatric and psychotherapeutic thinking that currently assume the cause of illness as lying within the patient's own experience. [Ruppert, 2008, p. 74]

While these were all interesting theories, I sensed that they were less than the experience they were attempting to describe. Given my belief that the only way to resolve our entangled relationships is to look to ourselves, I wondered what experiences lay within my own psyche.

So, back to my childhood. When my mother left my father we went to live with my grandparents. I simply adored my grandfather. I used to wait excitedly for him to come home from work each day when I would scramble on his knee as soon as I could, even when he was eating his supper. My favourite was when he had egg and chips. I would sit on his knee and dip my chip into his egg yolk and would get as close to him as I possibly could.

My grandfather had been deprived of a traditional education but used to tell me about the importance of self-education through reading. When I was six, he bought me a huge book of *Aesops Fables*, (written 620–560 BC). They were a selection of short stories about talking animals which each illustrate a particular moral and are meant as lessons for children. Each evening, he would read one of the stories to me and then would ask me what I really understood from the parable, what was the moral of the story, as in the race between the hare and the tortoise. He taught me always not to take things at face value. Only now do I realize that I was being taught philosophy from the age of six, the living system of my mind–brain being influenced by his mind–brain. It is important to recognize that it is not only traumatic and difficult experiences which are passed on, but strengths of character too. For me he was just Granddad; this is what I didn't know . . .

My handsome, slim, Irish Granddad was born in 1895 and was nineteen when the First World War broke out. I have traced his war records from his medals, but they are difficult to decipher. From 1914, he fought in three theatres of war; on one of his records he is marked as "dead". God alone knows what horrific experiences he went through in those years.

When he was twenty-one, he was drafted to the Battle of the Somme. There he was part of the artillery and fought in the trenches. A bullet went through his right shin on the first day.

The Battle of the Somme is described as the bloodiest day in the history of the British Army. By the end of the first day there were 64,470 casualties including 19,240 killed in action. An account from *La Bataille De La Somme 1916* (The Battle of the Somme) reads:

> Arms, legs, heads would stick out of the embankments in front of our dens, we could see torn off limbs and bodies sometimes covered with coats or tarpaulin because of the haunting sight of disfigured faces . . . Notwithstanding the scorching heat, no one thought to bury these bodies . . . [Laurent & Sutcliffe, 2006, pp. 100–101]

> Words can't accurately convey the anguish that a traumatised person experiences. It has an intensity that defies description. Many traumatized people feel that they live in a personal hell in which no other human could possibly share. [Levine & Frederick, 1997, p. 47]

My definition of psychological trauma and injury to the soul: In memory of my beloved grandfather, James Anthony Morris, 1895–1962

1st July, 1916. James, aged twenty-one, while advancing from the trenches, was wounded by a bullet which lodged in his right shin, leaving him unable to move. He lay in searing pain, blood pouring from his leg on to the muddy battlefield amongst the carnage of tens of thousands of dismembered and disfigured dead men with the accompanying nauseating stench of rotting corpses; the air was alive with the cries and screams of his wounded comrades crying for their mothers and girlfriends, or for death to quickly take them. He lay amongst 43,230 other casualties until darkness descended and the night engulfed him. It was twenty-four hours before he was picked up.

This is a story of living through the living bloody hell created by crazy men's thinking and sheer bloody madness. An attempt would be made later to define it in a text book as Post Traumatic Stress Syndrome.

Who has ever really defined madness properly?

CHAPTER EIGHT

War and peace

Diary extract

As my son, too, came out of his chaos period, the unseen hand of fate directed him to follow his inner guidance and took him off into an area of healing which I had never even considered. At the behest of his first therapist, he had become very interested in Bon Buddhism, which regards itself as a universal religion in the sense that its doctrines are true and valid for all humanity. He read avidly, and went to Buddhist groups. My son made his own appointment to see a medical practitioner who used acupuncture, herbs, and nutritional supplements. He still took an extremely small dose of the Abilify and regularly checked in with the doctor. I was happy that he had found his own path. It would be a long time before we discovered, to our horror, that his practitioner was, in fact, under investigation for malpractice. The hovering presence of our unwanted bullying guest could best be identified by my grim resolve to move on, i.e., my unspoken denial of the past few years. They were still difficult times but they were better.

The better times also helped me give up on my inner image of trying to climb the icy mountain of psychosis, dotted with men in white coats, looking for the non-existent fluttering flag that would represent a cure. I began to realize that, although this was at one time my internal metaphor, our present cultural symbol of psychosis may be likened to a cold, white, unconquerable mountain. When I opened my mind beyond this image, I realized that other societies might hold different beliefs, as psychosis has an incident rate that does not vary across the world.

I discovered that, as far back as 1485, in Edirne in Turkey, the Beyazit Kulesi, housed a complex of buildings that included a mosque, a school, guest house, mill, bakery, public bath, soup kitchen, and, most intriguingly of all, a psychiatric hospital. For almost four hundred years patients were treated with the sound of water, music, odorous scents, and various occupations, as well as medical knowledge and medicine.

> It has now been restored as a health museum showing life size figures illustrating various aspects of the therapy. In one there is a melancholic, someone suffering from "black love" or what we may call a broken heart. Another is labelled "Room for Treatment by Keeping Busy", what we might call occupational therapy. [Palin, 2007, p. 93]

This hospital, which actually cured patients, only closed its doors at the end of the nineteenth century because of Russian occupation.

So, my vision of a twenty-first century Integrative Psychiatric Day Clinic was not so innovative after all. Scott Peck, in *Further Along the Road Less Travelled* (1993), describes all diseases as "psycho-spiritual-socio-somatic" (p. 93). This model could be adopted for an integrative treatment of psychosis in which all parts of the treatment plan have equal importance. I would like to think there will be a time when the *psychological* disturbance will be treated with relationship based therapies and medication; the *spiritual* aspect of human nature will be addressed through encouraging the patient's systemic relationship to nature; the *social* context of the patient's life, including significant events and trauma in the family system, will be addressed through systemic/family constellation therapy; and the *somatic*, or physical, symptoms will be treated with the best of both conventional and alternative medicines.

It is interesting that, back in the days of the madhouses, there was more understanding of systemic natural laws than there is today. The word "lunatic" is derived from the Latin *luna*, for the moon. Early psychologists had no doubt about the moon's effect on our mental states. Extra staff were called into the asylums on the occasion of a full moon. The Lunacy Act 1824 stated that people were liable to go mad when the moon was full. But it is not just the mentally ill who are affected by a full moon; in 1998, a three-month psychological study of 1,200 inmates in the maximum security wing at Armley jail, Leeds, discovered a rise in violent incidents in the days before and after a full moon (Moore, 2007).

It is widely accepted among mental health carers that patients with psychotic disorders present more extreme symptoms at the time of a full moon. Psychosis is unique as an illness because it not only invites us consistently to recognize the power of our unconscious minds, but also reminds us that we are all subject to forces beyond our control, even beyond that of our own planet.

But, in my own life, I was far removed from thinking about the phases of the moon. I was now in the down-to-earth, hands-on, nitty-gritty, chaotic final phase of my mother's journey to meet her Maker. A journey that would be bedevilled for a while by hospital systems and their rules and inherent discrimination towards mental health problems.

Two and a half years had now passed since her initial diagnosis, and the final four months of her life present very dramatic physical deterioration. As the unrelenting progress of vascular dementia creates ever-increasing brain damage, she eventually suffers from the effects of a stroke. She falls, dislocates her shoulder, breaks her arm, and then deteriorates rapidly. Soon she becomes paralysed and incontinent. Removed from her home environment to hospital, she becomes totally confused, cannot speak up for herself, and becomes passive and submissive.

My mother's hospital experiences include bizarre incidents, such as being discharged by ambulance clutching a sealed brown envelope containing a note which quite clearly reads "Unfit for Discharge", and being refused admission to a private hospital ward on the technical grounds that "they didn't want her". At one point I was told to take her out of the hospital as they were short of beds, but when I returned to take her home, complete with details of the alternative care package I had managed to put together, they did a *volte-face* and told me that discharge was their decision and she could not leave. I felt battered by these experiences. Yet again, I am filling in the gaps in my mother's chaos narrative.

When my semi-paralysed, voiceless mother was discharged from a private hospital ward with notes reading "Unfit for Discharge", I can only conclude that this was done in the best interests of the hospital, not those of my mother. This is nothing short of insane and inhumane. I had been a daily visitor throughout her stay on the ward, and nobody informed me of this diagnosis. I was left powerless and voiceless yet again.

Again and again, I come to the conclusion that we are hard-wired to respond with empathy and kindness to visible physical distress at the same time as being equally hard-wired to turn away from non-physical, invisible, emotional and mental distress. It is as though, if we enter into the reciprocal interchange with someone suffering from emotional distress, then we, too, might be touched and drawn into seeing the deep pain that lies hidden from view in our collective hearts, minds, and souls; this deep pain that is currently labelled "mental illness".

After the miserable hospital experiences, and recognizing the only things that she now still knew was me, her GP, and her home, I arranged one-to-one, twenty-four hour private nursing care, backed up by additional nurses' visits and the attention of the loving, caring doctor. Every single thing had to be paid for privately, because she had savings and had dementia. The cost of these experiences was huge, not just in emotional and physical energy, but financially too. She spent her last months in an electronically operated bed by the patio windows overlooking her beautiful garden, waited on hand and foot.

When I realize that the end is nigh, I ask the doctor if he can arrange for her to go into the local hospice. He tells me he thinks he might be able to arrange it, as they might be changing their policy from only catering for cancer patients. I am horrified. I have worked twice for hospices. I know the ethos off by heart: *At the heart of the Hospice ethos is the commitment to treat the person, not the disease and to consider both the patient and family or carers, not just the person who is ill.*

He calls by the following day; he bows his head when he comes in. "I am very sorry, the hospice has refused her, they tell me they don't want to create a precedent by taking her as a stroke victim." When he goes, I cry. Even in her dying experience I experience discrimination. I cannot believe the hospice can exercise discrimination against someone now totally comatose. I wonder if "upstairs" thinks I haven't got the message that mentally ill people are discriminated against. I have run two private mental health hospitals, and now I have to run a hospice as well.

Even though she cannot move or speak, she can still see me, and I see reflected back in her eyes the reciprocal, active, deep loving bond between us. Most of my life I have been angry with her for her depression, but now I begin to realize she never wanted to be depressed. She was born in Middlesbrough, in 1926, ironically the year of the Great Depression. When the Second World War broke out, she was a young teenager and Granddad was an Air Raid Warden. She didn't talk about it much, except to say she used to hate it when she had just gone to sleep and the air raid siren started. She just wanted to stay in bed and resented being dragged out into the cold night air. One morning when she returned from the air raid shelter, her bedroom ceiling had fallen in, because along the road three houses had been bombed. She realized then how near the war was, and after that she did not want to stay in bed when she heard the sirens.

Those sirens that called the dreaming from their warm beds during the Second World War, heralding the deadliest conflict in human history, where over 60 million people died, the majority of them civilians. All this, and Granddad's traumatic experiences of the bloodiest day in the history of war hovering unspoken in her family background. Inherent insanity had been her world. How could she not suffer from feeling helpless and hopeless?

It is my mother's last afternoon on this earthly plane; a pale grey June day. My daughter goes to sit with her. I hear her soft, melodic voice reading one of John Betjeman's poems, "Miss J. Hunter Dunn, Miss J. Hunter Dunn, / Furnish'd and burnish'd by Aldershot sun".

My son, too, goes to sit with her. He has his prayer beads; I hear him chanting his Tibetan monks' prayers for the passing of the soul.

I am in awe of life and its beauty and the transformations that can occur.

Now, at last, I could simply acknowledge my mother's life for what it had been without wishing it had been different. As Hellinger says, if we want to connect with the source of life, we have to be connected with our parents first. "Whoever our parents are, however they behaved, they are the source of life for us" (Hellinger, 2002, p. 4). Life comes to us through them. "Then there are no more accusations, no more blaming. We just take what is given" (*ibid.*, p. 4).

I take a look at her just one more time, and take what is given, and then she is gone.

It is the funeral service. I hear the local vicar's words, "Janet, her only daughter, has requested that her mother's life is neither defined nor remembered by her life-long illness of depression, but by the perfection of her soul nature."

At the specific request of my son, at the end of the service, a local Buddhist stands by the coffin and reads the "Blessing for the Dead" from *The Tibetan Art of Living*, by Christopher Hansard (2001, p. 264).

> Good Friend, you have died,
> soon you are about
> to leave your body never to return.
> Your actions here are finished,
> You can take nothing with you on your way.
> All regrets, troubles and pain
> No longer have a claim upon you.
> Let your face receive the Clear Light.
> You are pure now, no blemish or stain.
> Hold on to your highest belief.
> It anchors you like a kite in the strong wind.
> Become unified with the divine.
> Let your spiritual friends guide you to unity.
> Good Friend, give blessings to all things.
> Compassion is with you on your way.

Reflections on war and peace

The predominant public perception of someone with a psychiatric diagnosis of psychosis, even in the twenty-first century, still invokes the image of a hapless victim with an abnormal brain and deviant crazy genes. These wretched souls, our beloved blameless sons, daughters, fathers, mothers, brothers, and sisters, then receive a prognosis of a life-long sentence of medication, often with severe and unpleasant side-effects. Not only that, but their behaviours and utterings are silenced by an unspoken but collective agreement that psychosis is the ultimate taboo.

Thus, society's generalized observations and opinions accurately reflect the lack of coherent theories in psychiatry, both in terms of causal evidence or effective treatments. Mercifully, there are new voices to be found within the ranks of psychiatry itself, in the form of The Critical Psychiatry Network, which is deeply sceptical about the reductionist claims of neuroscience to explain psychosis and other forms of emotional distress. They also recognize that there is no concrete evidence for antipsychotic long-term effectiveness. As yet, however, they offer no real alternative treatment plans.

In general, there seems to be scant evidence of any psychiatric hospital offering anything other than orthodox medication and scarce alternative or complementary therapies in the after-care programmes. This seems inconsistent with mainstream medicine in an era when 80% of cancer patients try alternative or complementary therapies at some stage after diagnosis (HRH the Prince of Wales, 2004). The link between mental health and physical health is now almost incontestable. Mind Week Survey 2000 reports that 88% of 550 people with mental health problems surveyed believe that there is a link between physical and mental health, and food is confirmed to be an important part of the mind–body relationship (www.mind.org.uk/foodandmood). The food and mood project celebrates its tenth anniversary this year, yet there appears to be no serious integration of it into mainstream mental health care. Over-specialization reigns as one of the curses of modern civilization.

The incidence of psychosis has been on the increase since the 1980s and 1990s due to cannabis-induced psychosis. There are approximately 25,000 new cases attributed to cannabis/skunk use. Even though the dangers of cannabis and its link to inducing psychosis have received extensive coverage in the media, this attention has not improved or had an impact on the quality of treatment plans, nor has the conspiracy of silence around psychosis been dispersed. Even with the raging debate about the reclassification of cannabis, there seems little interest from politicians. "Indeed to judge by the relative amounts of parliamentary time devoted to fox hunting and psychosis since 1997, MPs have been much more interested in the mental health of foxes that of its young citizens" (Murray, 2007).

It needs to be widely recognized that "psychosis is the end point of a long developmental pathway ... many psychotic patients experience distressing symptoms for long periods" before they are eligible for psychiatric support (Bentall, 2003, p. 509). Under the current interpretation of the Mental Health Act, waiting until they are a risk to others or themselves means that the government and the mental health profession are colluding in perpetuating the need for crises to arise; crises which may involve suicide, violent crimes, and even murder; crises which then adorn the front pages of the red-tops, reinforcing fear and discrimination.

The aim of the original legislation was to prioritize the protection of patients' rights, but over-protected them to such an extent that early and voluntary treatment has become virtually impossible. The psychotic patient is now suffering from the sins of logic of his forefathers, committed many years ago. However, society still prefers to dwell on medical diagnoses rather than look within itself to social diagnoses that require massive change.

This was the historical and cultural context against which my personal narrative of felt emotional responses was written. However, I am not just committed to describing these past experiences, but also to imagining possible new ways forward.

The ideal conditions for the development of genuine mental health care is one in which there is a recognition of its own imperfections. The formation of the Critical Psychiatry Network heralds that this time may now be ripe. Also, the new President of the Royal College of Psychiatrists, Professor Dinesh Bhugra, is using his inauguration to attack the state of Britain's acute psychiatric care system, saying, "I would not use them, and neither would I let any of my relatives do so" (*Observer*, 1, 29 June 2008). This is a clear message that our current level of psychiatric care is woefully inadequate, a message that families have known for decades and been unable to register in a useful way. Educational programmes, early intervention and preventive psychiatry rather than crisis management should become the new priorities in the interests of both the patient and the public and in the service of humanity.

In the telling of my story, I have had to display the courage to be vulnerable, so that I could step out from behind the curtain of shame which dominates the stage of psychotic illnesses. This is the first step which is required if there are ever to be any changes in treating psychosis with the dignity it deserves as an illness that has accompanied mankind since the beginning of time.

Before we are to take our place in society, we need to take a leaf from the book of the supporters of fox-hunting. We, in turn, need to lobby for our own cause of seeking recognition of the inherent suffering and lack of support for sufferers of psychosis and their families. First, however, we need to rip off the collective invisible elastoplasts that silence us and marginalize us. We need to reclaim our voices; our voices as a right to speak.

The inherent discrimination that seems common against all mental illnesses has recently hit the headlines through the author Terry Pratchett and his recent diagnosis of Alzheimer's. "Alzheimer's lacks 'heroic glamour' of cancer, says Pratchett" (Devlin, 2008). He draws attention to the fact that large amounts of money go to the illnesses with the highest profiles while other worthy causes suffer. For instance, donations to cancer charities increased when Kylie Minogue, the Australian singer, was diagnosed with the disease. Pratchett feels that he is speaking for the 700,000 other people with Alzheimer's who would not normally get a voice. He also challenges the mindset that there is no cure, and voices frustration that funding on research was three per cent of that for cancer (Devlin, 2008).

Dementia has recently shot to the top of the political agenda and marks a new awareness of another illness that robs people of their known personality. "Care for people with dementia will be transformed with the appointment of dementia advisers, better training for GPs and the establishment of memory services staffed by specialists to provide early diagnosis and treatment", Health Secretary Alan Johnson announced today. The first National Dementia Strategy, backed by £150 million over the first two years, will increase awareness of dementia, ensure early diagnosis and intervention, and radically improve the quality of care that people with the condition receive (www.Sdvs.org.uk 2009). This is an admirable model, but surely it is time to use a similar campaign to help the legions of young people affected by psychosis?

In *Key Concepts in Mental Health* (2005) David Pilgrim writes:

Relatives as a lobby group As relatives of those with mental health problems do not work together to advance their own personal liberation, they cannot be described as a full new social movement. [p. 88]

A full new social movement of relatives of sufferers of psychosis can only be born when we "come out" together, without any mediating influence, and "give voice" to one of the great untold stories of our time: the taboo of psychosis. If we can collectively tell our stories of similar experiences within the context of the current mental health system, we can emotionally bind and bond together and overcome some of the isolation and alienation that psychosis in the family brings.

Our voice could then become recognized and valued as a powerful influence in guiding mental health professionals to providing more effective and humane services. Facts bring us knowledge, but stories bring us wisdom. Only by listening to the stories of other wounded witnesses of psychotic people can we understand what is needed to ease their suffering, for it is not just expertise that is required, but compassion.

It has been a continuing test of endurance to write this book. In the writing, I had to make myself relive unpleasant memories and take myself back into distressing times I would rather forget. Concurrent with the experience of recognizing my suffering was also a need to want to run away from it, deny it, expel it, bury the memories and give myself over to the illusion that life could once again be predictable and pleasure focused.

It certainly has not been a time of mythic heroism. What I realize now is that the suffering cannot be left behind. I had no idea of the deep pain that lay in my soul; pain that I never even knew existed. I had no idea, until I began the constellation training, how emotional distress and suffering in a family is passed on. But this is not just a therapeutic insight. In Doris Lessing's latest book, *Alfred & Emily* (2008), the Nobel Prize winner explores the lives of her parents, both of them irrevocably damaged by the Great War. The war to end all wars. She is quoted on the cover as saying, "Here I still am, trying to get out from under that monstrous legacy." The legacy of trauma passed on through the bonding process. To illustrate her point, she quotes from D. H. Lawrence's *Lady Chatterley's Lover*:

And dimly she realised one of the great laws of the human soul: that when the emotional soul receives a wounding shock, which does not kill the body, the soul seems to recover as the body recovers. But this is only appearance. It is, really, only the mechanism of reassumed habit. Slowly, slowly the wound to the soul begins to make itself felt, like a bruise which only slowly deepens its terrible ache, till it fills all the psyche. And when we think we have recovered and forgotten, it is then that the terrible after-effects have to be encountered at their worst. [p. 151]

Could the terrible after-effects on the human soul encountered at their worst be in some ways linked to psychosis, an illness where we hear the poetic echoes of our culture and its suffering, a story too unbearable to hold its coherence?

So, I have used my own journey to recognize the common suffering that lies at the core of being human. When I accept my own pain, and that it is part of me and will always belong to me, then it strengthens instead of weakens me. Only now I have come to recognize that I do not come from a war-free generation. The trauma of war lived on through me. I suspect that we all carry vestiges of the trauma of the First and Second World Wars, and we can recognize it most easily by our desire not to dwell on it or remember it. The craziness of what people can do to each other, and have done, is beyond human comprehension. How these transgenerational traumatic experiences may contribute to the onset of psychosis could add another dimension to our understanding of the illness.

What I have learnt in the process is that there is no precise dividing line between normality and psychosis, just as there is no precise dividing line between them and us. When we are with them we often feel deep despair and frustration, but maybe it is just not their despair, but the multi-generational and collective despair that lies within the greater soul of humanity. For the psychotic individual reflects back to us how overwhelming the world we live in can be, and how difficult it is to maintain balance of the mind in an ever-changing sea of conflicting impulses, feelings, and desires.

In the telling of my story, I hope what will come out of it is what yet remains untold. For the more we tell, the more we become aware of what remains untold. The awareness of the hitherto untold importance of families in treatment plans is endorsed by the

World Fellowship for Schizophrenia, which has recently published *Families as Partners in Mental Health Care* (2007). Edwin Fuller Torrey wrote in *Surviving Schizophrenia*, in the preface to the fifth edition, "This is why all of us who have been touched by schizophrenia must work harder, why we all must advocate for those who cannot advocate for themselves. Only then will services improve".

I cannot really improve on these words. So I now offer encouragement for you to tell your story on the newly formed communal stage for families and friends of loved ones with psychosis, a stage with the curtains of shame firmly drawn back to give dignity and respect to our collective voice: a voice that needs to be recognized by mental health professionals as being crucial to early diagnosis, in acceptance of the fact that sufferers of untreated psychosis do not have insight into their own condition.

I wish I had something more tangible to offer you in these closing words. I wish I had something to offer that would help and would heal the inherent suffering that psychosis in the family brings.

In the meantime, across the invisible void that both separates us and connects us, I reach my hand out to yours.

P.S. I asked my son if he would like to say something for inclusion at the end of the book. His reply was "No comment."

One definition of trauma: an unspeakable experience. Unexplored beyond this point.

AFTERWORD

A part from my personal narrative, which, by definition, remains unique, I have to own that my ideas are not original. So many authors have gone before me and inspired me with their writing on giving dignity to mental illness.

I have been astounded at their similar perceptions to mine. When I have come across somebody else's way of looking at things that resonates with my own viewpoint, I have felt a lightening of spirit within me. In fact, I collected so many inspiring quotes I initially found it difficult to find my own voice, such was the breadth and depth of the material available.

I now feel it my obligation to openly name some of these authors, particularly those I have felt were collaborators in writing this book. For when two people, even when separated by the ages, think the same thoughts and sense the same feelings and understand each other, they are bonded. In the preparation of this book, I would like to name those no longer earthbound who have been with me in spirit; M. Scott Peck, a bedrock companion who has shaped my life; R. D. Laing, whose capacity for compassion and capriciousness inspired me; and Gregory Bateson, for expanding my thinking to systemical.

I would like to end this Afterword by saying that I am staggered by the amount of literature listed in the bibliography about psychosis, written from different, but often compassionate and humanistic, viewpoints in an attempt to shine a torch into the murky realms of madness and its treatment.

Compassion and cries from the soul are out there on the bookshelves, and yet I wonder, how does change really come about?

APPENDICES OF RESOURCES

The following is only a very basic list of some alternative resources to standard mental health services and charities. They contain no recommendations.

Appendix A: Orthomolecular and nutritional approaches to psychosis
Appendix B: Psychotherapy approaches for psychosis
Appendix C: Spiritual approaches
Appendix D: General resources for families

Orthomolecular and nutritional approaches to psychosis

Description

Orthomolecular medicine, pioneered since the 1950s by Dr Abram Hoffer and others, including Carl Pfeiffer, David Horrobin, Harold Foster, and Linus Pauling (who coined the term orthomolecular), describes the practice of using the most appropriate nutrients, including vitamins, minerals, and other essential compounds, in the most therapeutic amounts, according to an individual's particular biochemical requirements. Schizophrenia and psychoses are explained as a complex biochemical disorder that expresses itself in mental symptoms and originates from a vitamin-dependent condition. It is essential to discover the cause/s or triggers, which might be cerebral allergies; vitamin B-3 and B-6 dependencies; vitamin deficiencies; essential fatty acid deficiencies; mineral deficiencies, e.g., zinc; toxic reactions, e.g., to lead or to drugs.

Organizations

International Schizophrenia Foundation/International Society for Orthomolecular Medicine/Canadian Schizophrenia Foundation
Started in 1968 with international affiliates, dedicated to raising the levels of diagnosis, treatment and prevention of the schizophrenias

and allied disorders. Over 300 publications; promotes and supports research; quarterly *Journal of Orthomolecular Medicine*; quarterly *Nutrition and Mental Health* newsletter; annual international conferences; meetings, and regional conferences; branches answer thousands of enquiries from people seeking information and help.
16 Florence Avenue
Toronto
Canada M2N 1E9
+1 (416) 733 2117
centre@orthomed.org
www.orthomed.org
www.orthomed.com

The Institute for Optimum Nutrition (ION)/Brain Bio Centre
Avalon House
72 Lower Mortlake Road
Richmond
London TW9 2JY
+44 (0)20 8332 9600
www.brainbiocentre.com

The Ness Foundation
The Schizophrenia Association of Great Britain (SAGB) inspired and formed by Gwynneth Hemmings in 1970, campaigned for research for the biological causes of schizophrenia and for proper treatment for those afflicted. SAGB provided newsletters, support and information to its members and the public. Gwynneth and her supporters believe that psychiatric symptoms which people recognise as schizophrenia and psychoses, do not originate in the brain but derive from a pathological condition of the gut leading to malabsorption of nutrients which ultimately affects the chemistry of the brain. In 2007, Gwynneth retired, and the functions of the SAGB were transferred to The Ness Foundation, which carries on research and contact with members and supporters.
Ness House
Douchfour Business Centre
Inverness IV3 8GY
+44 (0)1463 220256
info@ness-foundation.org.uk
www.ness-foundation.org.uk

The Bright Spot for Health
Begun over thirty years ago by Dr Hugh Riordan, it is a biochemically based, nutritional medical centre, where patients are assessed
for the underlying causes of psychiatric problems, and a tailored
regimen and support is provided.
The Centre for Improvement of Human Functioning
3100 North Hillside Avenue
Wichita
Kansas 67219
USA
+1 (316) 682 3100
www.brightspot.org

Health Research Institute and Pfeiffer Treatment Centre
www.hriptc.org

Other websites

www.alternativementalhealth.com
www.orthomolecularvitamincentre.com
www.doctoryourself.com
www.biochemimbal-behaviour.com
www.mercola.com
www.4optimallife.com
www.nutritionvitamintherapy.com
www.mhnj.com

Books on orthomolecular psychiatry and natural healing for psychosis

A good resource for books in this category and others is
The Nutri Centre
7 Park Crescent
London W1B 1PF
Tel: +44 (0)845 602 6744
Bookshop and Library Tel: +44 (0)20 7322 2382
enq@nutricentre.com

Edelman, E. (2001). *Natural Healing for Schizophrenia* (3rd edn). Eugene, OR: Borage Books.

Foster, H. D. (2003). *What Really Causes Schizophrenia.* www.hdfoster.com

Hoffer, A. (2004). *Healing Schizophrenia; Complementary Vitamin and Drug Treatments.* Canada: CCMN Press.

Hoffer, A. (2005). *Adventures in Psychiatry: The Scientific Memoirs of Abram Hoffer.* Canada: KOS.

Hoffer, A., & Osmond, H. (1974). *How to Live with Schizophrenia.* New York: Carol, 1992.

Hoffer, A., & Walker, M. (1996). *Putting it All Together: The New Orthomolecular Nutrition.* New Canaan, CT: Keats.

Holford, P. (2003). *Optimum Nutrition for the Mind.* London: Judy Piatkus.

Horrobin, D. (2001). *The Madness of Adam & Eve: How Schizophrenia Shaped Humanity.* London: Bantam.

Marohn, S. (2003). *The Natural Medicine Guide to Schizophrenia.* Charlottesville, VA: Hampton Roads.

Pfeiffer, C. C. (1987). *Nutrition and Mental Illness; An Orthomolecular Approach to Balancing Body Chemistry.* Vermont, VA: Healing Arts Press.

Schuyler, W. L., Gaby, A. R., Austin, S. N. D., Brown, D. J., Wright, J. V., & Duncan, A. (1999). *The Natural Pharmacy: Complete Home Reference to Natural Medicine.* London: Random House.

Nutritional approach

Changing Diets, Changing Minds: How Food Affects Mental Health and Behaviour, by C. Van de Weyer. Food & Mental Health (ISBN: 1-903060–40-0) 128 pp, 2006.

The report pulls together the published evidence linking what we eat to how we feel, from foetal brain development to adolescent behaviour through to Alzheimer's disease. Due to both the quantity and quality of the evidence (epidemiological, physiological, and through randomized control trials), the report proposes that the changes to the food system seen in the past century may be partly responsible for the rise in mental health and behavioural problems at the same time. Specific mental diseases discussed include: attention deficit hyperactivity disorder (ADHD), depression, schizophrenia, and dementia (particularly Alzheimer's disease).

Copies are available from Sustain, 94 White Lion Street, London N1 9PF. Tel: +44 (0)20 7837 2250.

Psychotherapeutic approaches to psychosis

Human Givens approach

Description

This approach proposes that psychosis is the last phase in a continuum of emotional patterns in the brain that progress from stress to depression to psychosis. People in psychosis are considered to be trapped in the Rapid Eye Movement (REM) state, a separate state of consciousness with dreamlike qualities where waking reality is processed through the dreaming brain.

Organizations

Mindfields College
Chalvington
East Sussex
BN27 3TD
Tel: +44 (0)1232 81440
info@mindfields.org.uk
www.mindfields.org.uk

Websites

www.humangivens.com
www.hgfoundation.com
www.hgi.org.uk

Books

Griffin, J., & Tyrrell, I. (2003). *Human Givens: A New Approach to Emotional Health & Clear Thinking*. Chelvington: HG Publishing.
Griffin, J., & Tyrrell, I. (2004). *Dreaming Reality: How Dreaming Keeps Us Sane, or Can Drive Us Mad*. Chelvington: HG Publishing.

Process oriented psychology

Description

Process Work was developed by Jungian analyst Arnold Mindell in the 1970s, when Mindell began researching illness as a meaningful expression of the unconscious mind, and works with extreme and altered states of consciousness.

Organizations

Research Society for Process Oriented Psychology UK
The national forum and organising body for process work in the UK.
Interchange Studios
Hampstead Town Hall Centre
213 Haverstock Hill
London NW3 4QP
(Limited Company: 4794982. Registered Charity: 1107684)
Tel: 08704 295256
E-mail: contact@rspopuk.com
Website: www.rspouk.com

Jean-Claude and Arlene Augergon
They work with individuals and organizations and teach process work in the UK and internationally.
Website: www.processwork-audergon.com

Philadelphia Association
This organization was founded in 1965 by R. D. Laing and others to challenge accepted ways of understanding and treating mental and emotional suffering. They have community households where people with serious emotional difficulties can live with others for substantial periods of time and try to make sense of their difficulties and live more productive lives. They also offer individual psychotherapy, psychotherapy training programmes, and introductory courses.
4 Marty's Yard
17 Hampstead High Street
London NW3 1QW
+44 (0)20 7794 2652
E-mail: office@philadelphia-association.org.uk
Website: www.philadelphia-association.org.uk

Spiritual approaches

Spirit release

Description

Spirit release is based on the premise that, after a person dies, if the soul does not go to the Light to enter the spirit world properly, it stays mentally attached to the earth plane and can attach to a person or place. One may be vulnerable to spirit attachment due to illness, injury, drugs, or emotional disturbance. Spirit attachment is not recognized as a psychiatric diagnosis, and this approach challenges the established view of consciousness as a biological phenomenon, and by-product of brain activity, and proposes that consciousness can survive bodily death. It is considered that in schizophrenia, many of the voices heard by patients might be due to attached spirits.

Organizations

Spirit Release Foundation
Website: www.spiritrelease.com

Spiritual emergence/spiritual crisis

Description

The term "spiritual emergency" was coined by Stanislov Grof and proposes that psychotic experiences are a spiritual breakdown which has the potential for a positive spiritual breakthrough, or "spiritual emergence".

Organizations

Spiritual Crisis Network
Their aim is to raise awareness and understanding about spiritual crisis and for individuals and professionals to find out what support is available. They are developing a website and central reference point.
Spiritual Crisis Network
PO Box 303
Stroud GL6 1BF
UK
Website: www.spiritualcrisisnetwork.org.uk

Spiritual Competency Resource Centre
Spiritual Competency Resource Centre provides access to online resources that enhance the cultural sensitivity of mental health professionals. Spirituality is now accepted as an important component of cultural competence for mental health professionals. These resources include online courses, guides to Internet resources, and articles. Proponents include David Lukoff, Dr Rufus May, and Dr Nikki Crowley.
Website: www.spiritualcompetency.com

Books

Grof, C., & Grof, S. (1990). *The Stormy Search for the Self*. Los Angeles, CA.
Nelson, J. E. (1994). *Healing the Split: Integrating Spirit Into Our Understanding of the Mentally Ill*. Albany, NY: State University of New York Press.

General resources for families

Psychotherapy

United Kingdom Council for Psychotherapy
The UKCP exists to promote and maintain the profession of psychotherapy and the highest standards in the practice of psychotherapy
throughout the United Kingdom, for the benefit of the public. It
also has a "find a practitioner" facility through their website.
2nd Floor Edward House
2 Wakley Street
London EC1V 7LT
Tel: 020 7014 9955
Fax: 020 7014 9977
E-mail: info@psychotherapy.org.uk
www.psychotherapy.org.uk

British Association for Counselling and Psychotherapy
The UK's professional membership association for counsellors
and psychotherapists, BACP is the largest and broadest body
within the sector. Through its work, BACP ensures that it meets its
remit of public protection while also developing and informing its
members. Its work with large and small organizations within the

sector ranges from advising schools on how to set up a counselling service, assisting the NHS on service provision, working with voluntary agencies, and supporting independent practitioners. BACP participates in the development of counselling and psychotherapy at an international level.

You can "find a therapist" through their website.
British Association for Counselling and Psychotherapy
BACP House
15 St John's Business Park
Lutterworth
Leicestershire LE17 4HB
UK
Tel: +44 (0)20 7014 9955
Fax: 020 7014 9977
E-mail: info@psychotherapy.org.uk
Website: www.psychotherapy.org.uk

Autogenic therapy

Description

Autogenic therapy developed in 1932 and, with its roots firmly based in medicine, is probably the most effective non-drug technique for dealing with stress ever developed in the West and is learnt in only eight sessions. Autogenic means self-generating, so that the client is empowered through learning a series of simple, easily learnt mental exercises which link mind and body, which they can use at any time and anywhere. In the autogenic state, the autonomic nervous system, which is normally beyond the realm of conscious control, moves from the sympathetic, which is concerned with arousal, stress, and flight, to the parasympathetic, which allows recuperation and restoration. This enables the body to move towards its natural state of homeostasis, supporting the immune system, promoting healing processes, and reducing anxiety and stress.

Organizations

The British Autogenic Society (BAS) is the professional and educational organization for Autogenic Therapists in the United Kingdom.

The Royal London Homeopathic Hospital
Great Ormond Street
London WC1N 3HR
+44 (0)20 7391 8908
E-mail: admin@autogenic-therapy.org.uk
Website: www.autogenic-therapy.org.uk

Family constellation therapy

Family constellation therapy, pioneered by psychotherapist and philosopher Bert Hellinger, identifies how, in a family, there are certain loyalties and fates which are transmitted down the generations through the operation of unconscious family consciences. Influences in the family system can have negative effects on family members for two, three, or more generations, causing a wide variety of life problems, which can also manifest as physical or mental illnesses, including psychosis.

There are many family constellation therapists and books which can be found online.

Professor Franz Ruppert

Professor Dr Franz Ruppert is Professor of Psychology at the University of Applied Sciences in Munich, Germany. Since 1995, he has focused on family constellation therapy work and specifically on the causes of psychosis, schizophrenia, and other forms of severe mental illness. He has combined with this his interest in bonding and attachment theories and modern trauma work.

Professor Ruppert is based in Munich, but comes to speak and train in the UK with Constellations Work Trainings.

His publications include: *Trauma, Bonding and Family Constellations: Understanding and Healing Injuries of the Soul.*
Website: www.franz-ruppert.de
Website: www.constellationswork.co.uk

Loving Someone in Psychosis (LSIP)

Loving Someone in Psychosis is a new charity which aims to help families help their loved ones. The charity's aim is to counteract the isolation and alienation felt as family and friends of sufferers of psychosis. Not only do they feel that they have to cope with non-negotiable beliefs of their loved ones and the associated stigma, they also share experiences of powerlessly watching their loved ones suffer and deteriorate, often without recourse to treatment until they reach crisis point.

LSIP will offer support networks and social events. Their mission is to promote the voice of the family and friends "to help us help our loved ones".

E-mail: info@lsip.org.uk

Website: www.lsip.org.uk

Books

Arieti, S. (1981). *Understanding and Helping the Schizophrenic: A Guide for Family and Friends*. Harmondsworth: Penguin.

Frogatt, D., Fadden, G., Johnson, D., Leggatt, M., & Shankar, R. (Eds.) (2007). *Families as Partners in Mental Health Care: A Guidebook for Implementing Family Work*. Toronto, Canada: World Fellowship for Schizophrenia and Allied Disorders. www.world-schizophrenia.org

Mueser, K., & Gingerich, S. (1994). *Coping with Schizophrenia; A Guide for Families*. Oakland, CA: New Harbinger

Sanghera, S. (2008). *If You Don't Know Me By Now* London: Viking.

Torrey, E. F. (2006). *Surviving Schizophrenia: A Manual for Families, Patients and Providers* (5th edn). New York: Collins.

REFERENCES

American Psychiatric Association (2000). *Diagnostic and Statistical Manual of Mental Disorders—DSM-IV* (4th edn). Washington, DC: American Psychiatric Association.

Arieti, S. (1981). *Understanding and Helping the Schizophrenic; A Guide for Family & Friends*. Harmondsworth: Penguin.

Bateson, G. (1972). *Steps to an Ecology of Mind*. Chicago, IL: University of Chicago Press.

Bennett, A. (2005). *Untold Stories*. London: Faber & Faber and Profile Books.

Bentall, R. (2003). *Madness Explained: Psychosis and Human Nature*. London: Penguin.

Broks, P. (2003). *Into the Silent Land: Travels in Neuropsychology*. London: Atlantic Books.

Burston, D. (1996). *The Wing of Madness: The Life and Work of R. D. Laing*. MA: Harvard University Press.

Campbell, J. (1973). *Myths to Live By*. London: Souvenir Press.

Cooper, D. (1967). *Psychiatry and Anti-Psychiatry*. St Albans: Paladin.

Day, P. (2002). *The Mind Game*. Tonbridge: Credence Publications.

De Laszlo, V. (Ed.) (1990). *The Basic Writings of C. G. Jung*. Princeton, NJ: Princeton University Press.

Devlin, K. (2008). Alzheimer's lacks "heroic glamour" of cancer, says Pratchett. *Daily Telegraph*, 14 March.

Dorman, D. (2003). *Dante's Cure: A Journey Out of Madness*. New York: Other Press.

Eliot, T. S. (2008). *Four Quartets 1: Burnt Norton*. www.tristan.icom43. net/quartets/notes.html. Accessed 9 April 2008.

Ellenburger, H. (1970). *The Discovery of the Unconscious*. New York: Basic Books.

Etherington, K. (2004). *Becoming a Reflexive Researcher; Using Ourselves in Research*. London: Jessica Kingsley.

Faithfull, P. (2002). *Basic Facts About Lunatics in England and Wales for Family Historians*. Bury: Federation of Family History Societies.

Foucault, M. (1988). *Madness and Civilization: A History of Insanity in the Age of Reason*. New York: Vintage Books.

Frank, A. (1995). *The Wounded Storyteller: Body, Illness, and Ethics*. Chicago, IL: University of Chicago Press.

Frith, C., & Johnstone, E. (2003). *Schizophrenia: A Very Short Introduction*. Oxford: Oxford University Press.

Frogatt, D., Fadden, G., Johnson, D. L., Leggatt, M., & Shankar, R. (Eds.) (2007). *Families as Partners in Mental Health Care: A Guidebook for Implementing Family Work*. Toronto, Canada: World Fellowship for Schizophrenia and Allied Disorders. www.world-schizophrenia.org.

Goffman, E. (1963). *Stigma: Notes on the Management of Spoiled Identity*. Upper Saddle River, NJ: Prentice-Hall.

Gutting, G. (2005). *Foucault: A Very Short Introduction*. Oxford: Oxford University Press.

Hansard, C. (2001). *The Tibetan Art of Living*. London: Hodder & Stoughton.

Hawkes, N. (2008). New laws to govern alternative medicine. *The Times*, 5 January.

Hellinger, B. (2002). Bert Hellinger: the Alpha. *Systemic Solutions Bulletin*, 3: 4.

Hellinger, B., Weber, G., & Beaumont, H. (1998). *Love's Hidden Symmetry: What Makes Love in Relationships*. Phoenix, AZ: Zeig, Tucker.

Hillman, J., & Ventura, M. (1993). *We've had a Hundred Years of Psychotherapy and the World's Getting Worse*. New York: Harper Collins.

Hobson, P. (2002). *The Cradle of Thought; Exploring the Origins of Thinking*. London: Pan.

Hoffer, A. (1999). *Orthomolecular Treatment for Schizophrenia*. Lincolnwood, IL: Keats.

HRH the Prince of Wales (2004). HRH calls for more research into complementary therapies (23 June). www.princeofwales.gov.uk/newsandgallery/news. Accessed 30 March 2008.

James, O. (2004). Family therapy. *Observer*, 25 April 2004.

Johannessen, J., Martindale, B., & Cullberg, J. (Eds) (2006). *Evolving Psychosis: Different Stages, Different Treatments*. The International Society for the Psychological Treatment of Schizophrenias and other Psychoses. London: Routledge.

Kushner, H. (1981). *When Bad Things Happen to Good People*. New York: Schocken.

Laing, R. D. (1959). *The Divided Self*. London: Tavistock.

Laing, R. D., & Esterson, A. (1964). *Sanity, Madness and the Family*. Harmondsworth: Penguin.

Laurence, J. (2003). *Pure Madness: How Fear Drives the Mental Health System*. New York: Routledge.

Laurent, A., & Sutcliffe, C. (2006). *La Bataille De La Somme 1916*. Amiens, France: Martelle Editions.

Levine, P., & Frederick, A. (1997). *Waking the Tiger; Healing Trauma*. California: North Atlantic Books.

Marohn, S. (2003). *The Natural Medicine Guide to Schizophrenia*. Charlottesville, VA: Hampton Roads.

Mental Health Care (2008). Family relationships & schizophrenia. www.mentalhealthcare.org.uk/content/?id=32, accessed February 2008.

Mental Health Foundation (2006). *Feeding Minds*. www.mhf.org.uk/publications/?EntryId5=38571&char=F. Accessed March 2008.

Mindell, A. (1991). *City Shadows; Psychological Interventions in Psychiatry*. Harmondsworth: Arkana.

Mollon, P. (2000). *Ideas in Psychoanalysis: The Unconscious*. Cambridge: Icon.

Moncrieff, J. (2007). *The Myth of the Chemical Cure: A Critique of Psychiatric Drug Treament*. Basingstoke: Palgrave Macmillan.

Moore, V. (2007). More babies born. More crime. More suicides. Now scientists try to explain why we're all moonstruck. www.dailymail.co.uk/pages/live/articles/news/news.html?in_article_id=431239&in_page_id=1770. Accessed January 2008.

Moustakas, C., & Douglass, B. G. (1985). Heuristic inquiry. The internal search to know. *Journal of Humanistic Psychology*, 25(3): 39–55.

Mueser, K., & Gingerich, S. (1994). *Coping with Schizophrenia; A Guide for Families*. Oakland, CA: New Harbinger.

Murray, R. (2007). Teenage schizophrenia is the issue, not legality. www.independent.co.uk/opinion/commentators/robin-murray-teenage-schizophrenia-is-the-issue-not-legality-440670.html. Accessed 30 March 2008.

Neenan, M., & Dryden, W. (2002). *Cognitive Behaviour Therapy: An A–Z of Persuasive Arguments*. London: Whurr.

Palin, M. (2007). *Michael Palin: New Europe*. London: Orion.

Peck, M. S. (1983). *The Road Less Travelled; The New Psychology of Love, Traditional Values and Spiritual Growth*. London: Arrow.

Peck, M. S. (1993). *Further Along the Road Less Travelled; The Unending Journey Towards Spiritual Growth*. London: Simon & Schuster.

Pfeiffer, C. (1987). *Nutrition and Mental Illness; An Orthomolecular Approach to Balancing Body Chemistry*. Vermont, VA: Healing Arts Press.

Pilgrim, D. (2005). *Key Concepts in Mental Health*. London: Sage.

Pirsig, R. (1999). *Zen and the Art of Motorcycle Maintenance*. London: Vintage.

Remen, R. (2006). *Kitchen Table Wisdom; Stories that Heal* (10th anniversary edn). New York: Riverhead.

Rossi, E. (2002). *The Psychobiology of Gene Expression: Neuroscience and Neurogenesis in Hypnosis and Healing Arts*. Norton Professional Books. www.ernestrossi.com/about_psychotherapy_of_gene_expression.htm. Accessed March 2008.

Ruppert, F. (2002). Psychosis & schizophrenia: disturbed bonding in the family system. *Systemic Solutions Bulletin*, 3: 15–25.

Ruppert, F. (2008). *Trauma, Bonding & Family Constellations: Understanding and Healing Injuries of the Soul*. Frome: Systemic Constellations.

Sarno, J. (1998). *The Mindbody Prescription; Healing the Body, Healing the Pain*. New York: Warner.

Sheldrake, R., & Beaumont, H. (2002). In conversation on the subject of practical research. *Systemic Constellations Bulletin*, 3: 57–58.

Stafford District Voluntary Services. *Landmark Strategy to Transform Dementia Services*. www.sdvs.org.uk/headlines/?p=2062. Accessed 19 March 2009.

Szasz, T. (1974). *The Myth of Mental Illness*. New York: Harper.

Tallis, F. (2002). *Hidden Minds; A History of the Unconscious*. London: Profile.

The Teresian Carmelites of the Anglo-Irish Province (2004). *Mount Carmel: A Review of the Spiritual Life*, 52(2): April–June.

Torrey, E. F. (1980). *Schizophrenia and Civilization.* New York: Jason Aronson.

Torrey, E. F. (2006). *Surviving Schizophrenia; A Manual for Families, Patients and Providers* (5th edn). New York: Collins.

Wallcraft, J. (1998). *Healing Minds: A Report on Current Research, Policy and Practice Concerning The Use of Complementary and Alternative Therapies for a Wide Range of Mental Health Problems.* London: The Mental Health Foundation.

Wilber, K. (2001). *Grace and Grit: Spirituality and Healing in the Life and Death of Treya Killam Wilber.* Boston, MA: Shambala.

Winnicott, D. (1965). *The Family and Individual Development.* Abingdon: Routledge.

World Health Organisation Regional Office for Europe (2002). *European Health Report 2002.* Geneva: WHO.

BIBLIOGRAPHY

Bennett-Goleman, T. (2001). *Emotional Alchemy: How the Mind can Heal the Heart*. London: Rider.

Bettelheim, B. (1991). *Freud and Man's Soul*. London: Penguin.

Bird, J., & Pinch, C. (2002). *Autogenic Therapy: Self-help for Mind and Body*. Dublin: Newleaf.

Blackmore, S. (2003). *Consciousness: An Introduction*. London: Hodder and Stoughton.

Bolton, G., Field, V., & Thomson, K. (2006). *Writing Works: A Resource Handbook for Therapeutic Writing Workshops and Activities*. London: Jessica Kingsley.

Bolton, G., Howlett, S., Lago, C., & Wright, J. K. (2004). *Writing Cures*. Hove: Brunner-Routledge.

Braden, G. (2007). *The Divine Matrix: Bridging Time, Space, Miracles, and Belief*. London: Hay House.

Brady, M. (Ed.) (2003). *The Wisdom of Listening*. Boston, MA: Wisdom.

Burns, T. (2006). *Psychiatry: A Very Short Introduction*. New York: Oxford University Press.

Clarke, R. (1995). *The Cure for All Diseases*. Chula Vista, CA: New Century.

Cousins, N. (1979). *Anatomy of an Illness; As Perceived by the Patient*. New York: W. W. Norton.

Dossey, L. (2001). *Healing Beyond the Body: Medicine and the Infinite Reach of the Mind*. MA: Shambala.

Dryden, W. (1996). *Handbook of Individual Therapy*. London: Sage.

Dryden, W., & Mytton, J. (1999). *Four Approaches to Counselling and Psychotherapy*. London: Routledge.

Dyer, W. (2001). *There is a Spiritual Solution to Every Problem*. London: Harper Collins.

Edelman, E. (1996). *Natural Healing for Schizophrenia and Other Common Mental Disorders*. Eugene, OR: Borage Books.

Edinger, E. (1985). *Anatomy of the Psyche: Alchemical Symbolism in Psychotherapy*. Peru, IL: Open Court.

Etherington, K. (Ed.) (2003). *Trauma, the Body and Transformation; A Narrative Enquiry*. London: Jessica Kingsley.

Fletcher, A. (2001). *The Art of Looking Sideways*. London: Phaidon.

Foster, H. (2004). *What Really Causes Schizophrenia*. www.hdfoster.com. Accessed March 2004.

Foundation for Inner Peace (1975). *A Course in Miracles*. Harmondsworth: Penguin.

Frank, A. (2002). *At the Will of the Body: Reflections on Illness*. New York: First Mariner.

Frank, U. (2003). *The River Never Looks Back: Historical and Practical Foundations of Bert Hellinger's Family Constellations*. Heidelberg: Carl-Auer-Systeme Verlag.

Frank, U. (2005). *In My Mind's Eye: Family Constellations in Individual Therapy and Counselling* (2nd edn). Heidelberg: Carl-Auer-Systeme Verlag.

Frayn, M. (2006). *The Human Touch; Our Part in the Creation of the Universe*. London: Faber and Faber.

Goldstein, N., Martin, S., & Cialdini, R. (2007). *Yes! 50 Secrets From The Science Of Persuasion*. London: Profile.

Goleman, D. (2007). *Social Intelligence*. London: Arrow.

Gordon, P. (1999). *Face to Face: Therapy as Ethics*. London: Constable.

Green, L. (1978). *Relating: An Astrological Guide on Living with Others on a Small Planet*. York Beach, ME: Samuel Weiser, Inc.

Griffin, J., & Tyrrell, I. (2003). *Human Givens: A New Approach to Emotional Health & Clear Thinking*. Chalvington: HG Publishing.

Griffin, J., & Tyrrell, I. (2004). *Dreaming Reality: How Dreaming Keeps Us Sane, or Can Drive Us Mad*. Chalvington: HG Publishing.

Grof, C., & Grof, S. (1990). *The Stormy Search for the Self; Understanding and Living with Spiritual Emergency*. Los Angeles, CA: Jeremy Thatcher.

Heller, T., Reynolds, J., Gomm, R., Muston, R., & Pattison, S. (Eds.) (1996). *Mental Health Matters: A Reader*. Basingstoke: Palgrave.

Hellinger, B. (2006). *No Waves Without the Ocean*. Heidelberg, Germany: Carl-Auer-Systeme Verlag.

Hellinger, B., & ten Hovel, G. (1999). *Acknowledging What Is: Conversations with Bert Hellinger*. Phoenix, AZ: Zeig, Tucker.

Hoffer, A. (2004). *Healing Schizophrenia: Complementary Vitamin & Drug Treatments*. Canada: CCNM Press.

Hoffer, A. (2005). *Adventures in Psychiatry; The Scientific Memoirs of Dr. Abram Hoffer*. Canada: KOS.

Hoffer, A., & Osmond, H. (1974). *How to Live With Schizophrenia*. New York: Carol.

Hoffer, A., & Walker, M. (1996). *Putting it All Together: The New Orthomolecular Nutrition*. New Canaan, CT: Keats.

Holford, P. (2003). *Optimum Nutrition for the Mind*. London: Judy Piatkus.

Horrobin, D. (2001). *The Madness of Adam & Eve; How Schizophrenia Shaped Humanity*. London: Bantam.

Hunt, C., & Sampson, F. (2006). *Writing: Self and Reflexivity*. Hampshire: Palgrave Macmillan.

Inge, W. (1969). *Mysticism in Religion*. London: Rider.

Ingerman, S. (1991). *Soul Retrieval: Mending the Fragmented Self*. San Francisco, CA: HarperCollins.

Jacobs, M. (1998). *Psychodynamic Counselling in Action*. London: Sage.

James, O. (2002). *They F*** You Up: How to Survive Family Life*. London: Bloomsbury.

Johnson, R. (1989). *Inner Work: Using Dreams and Active Imagination for Personal Growth*. New York: Harper & Row.

Johnson, R. (1993). *Owning Your Own Shadow*. New York: HarperCollins.

Jones, A. (2007). *The Road He Travelled: The Revealing Biography of M. Scott Peck*. London: Rider.

Joy, C. (Ed.) (1947). *The Spiritual Life: Selected Writings of Albert Schweitzer*. Boston, MA: Beacon Press.

Jung, C. (1933). *Jung: Modern Man in Search of a Soul*. Kegan Paul, Trench, Trubner [reprinted London: Routledge Classics, 2001].

Jung, C. (1978). *Man and his Symbols*. London: Picador.

Kampenhout, D. (2001). *Images of the Soul: The Workings of the Soul in Shamanic Rituals and Family Constellations*. Heidelberg: Carl-Auer-Systeme Verlag.

Katie, B. (2002). *Loving What Is: Four Questions That Can Change Your Life*. London: Rider.

Kopp, S. (1976). *If You Meet the Buddha on the Road, Kill Him*. New York: Bantam.

Laing, A. (1994). *R. D. Laing: A Life*. Stroud: Sutton.

Laing, R. D. (1967). *The Politics of Experience and The Bird of Paradise*. Harmondsworth: Penguin.

Lessing, D. (2005). *Time Bites*. London: Harper Perennial.

Levin, M. (2000). *Spiritual Intelligence: Awakening the Power of your Spirituality and Intuition*. London: Hodder and Stoughton.

Levitt, S., & Dubner, S. (2005). *Freakonomics*. London: Allen Lane.

Lewis, C. S. (1940). *The Problem of Pain*. London: Geoffrey Bles [reprinted Fount Paperbacks, 1998].

Luthe, W. (2001). *Autogenic Therapy, Volume IV: Research and Theory*. London: British Autogenic Society.

Luthe, W. (2001). *Autogenic Therapy, Volume V: Dynamics of Autogenic Neutralization*. London: British Autogenic Society.

Luthe, W. (2001). *Autogenic Therapy, Volume VI: Treatment with Autogenic Neutralization*. London: British Autogenic Society.

Luthe, W., & Schultz, J. (2001). *Autogenic Therapy, Volume I: Autogenic Methods*. London: British Autogenic Society.

Luthe, W., & Schultz, J. (2001). *Autogenic Therapy, Volume III: Applications in Psychotherapy*. London: British Autogenic Society.

Madelung, E., & Innecken, B. (2004). *Entering Inner Images: A Creative Use of Constellations in Individual Therapy, Counselling, Groups and Self-Help*. Heidelberg: Carl-Auer-Systeme.

Martel, Y. (2002). *The Life of Pi*. Edinburgh: Canongate.

May, G. (2005). *The Dark Night of the Soul: A Psychiatrists Explores the Connection Between Darkness and Spiritual Growth*. San Francisco, CA: Harper.

McMillin, D. (1995). *Cases in Schizophrenia*. Virginia Beach, VA: ARE Press.

McTaggart, L. (2003). *The Field: The Quest for the Secret Force of the Universe*. London: HarperCollins.

Mearns, D., & Thorne, B. (1998). *Person-Centred Counselling in Action*. London: Sage.

Murphy, E. (1991). *After the Asylums; Community Care for People with Mental Illness*. London: Faber and Faber.

Murphy, J. (2000). *The Power of Your Subconscious Mind*. London: Pocket Books.

Nelson, J. E. (1994). *Healing the Split: Integrating Spirit Into Our Understanding of the Mentally Ill*. Albany, NY: State University of New York Press.

Nouwen, H. (1994). *The Wounded Healer*. London: Darton, Longman and Todd.

Nouwen, H. (2001). *Turning My Mourning into Dancing; Finding Hope in Hard Times*. Nashville, TN: W. Publishing Group.

Payne, J. (2005). *The Healing of Individuals, Families and Nations*. Findhorn: Findhorn.

Payne, J. (2006). *The Language of the Soul: Healing with Words of Truth*. Findhorn: Findhorn.

Payne, J. (2007). *The Presence of the Soul: Transforming Your Life Through Soul Awareness*. Findhorn: Findhorn.

Peck, S. (1997). *The Road Less Travelled and Beyond; Spiritual Growth in an Age of Uncertainty*. London: Rider.

Perry, J. (2005). *The Far Side of Madness* (2nd edn). Putnam, CT: Spring Publications.

Pert, C. (1997). *Molecules of Emotion; Why You Feel the Way You Feel*. London: Simon & Schuster.

Phillips, A. (2005). *Going Sane*. London: Penguin.

Pirsig, R. (2006). *Lila: An Inquiry into Morals* (the sequel to *Zen and the Art of Motorcycle Maintenance*). Richmond: Alma Books.

Radin, D. (2006). *Entangled Minds: Extrasensory Experiences in a Quantum Reality*. New York: Paraview & Pocket Books.

Ramsey, J. (1997). *Alchemy: The Art of Transformation*. London: Thorsons.

Rogers, C. (1967). *A Therapist's View of Psychotherapy: On Becoming a Person*. London: Constable.

Rowan, J. (1993). *The Transpersonal: Psychotherapy and Counselling*. London: Routledge.

Schuyler, W., Gaby, A., Austin, S., Brown, D., Wright, J., & Duncan, A. (1999). *The Natural Pharmacy: Complete Home Reference to Natural Medicine*. London: Random House.

Searle, J. (1997). *The Mystery of Consciousness*. London: Granta Books.

Searles, H. (1960). *The Nonhuman Environment: In Normal Development in Schizophrenia*. Madison, WI: International Universities Press.

Shepherd, G., Murray, A., & Muijen, M. (1994). *Relative Values: The Differing Views of Users, Family Carers & Professionals on Services for People with Schizophrenia in the Community*. London: The Sainsbury Centre for Mental Health.

Somers, B., & Gordon-Brown, I. (2002). *Journey in Depth: A Transpersonal Perspective*. UK: Archive.

Storr, A. (1979). *The Art of Psychotherapy*. Oxford: Butterworth-Heinemann.

Symington, N. (1986). *The Analytic Experience: Lectures from Tavistock*. London: Free Association.

Szasz, T. (2007). *Coercion as Cure: A Critical History of Psychiatry*. New Brunswick, NJ: Transaction Publishers.

Szasz, T. (2008). *Psychiatry: The Science of Lies*. New York: Syracuse University Press.

Thorne, B. (2002). *The Mystical Power of Person-Centred Therapy: Hope Beyond Despair*. London: Whurr.

Tolle, E. (1999). *The Power of Now: A Guide to Spiritual Enlightenment*. London: Hodder & Stoughton.

Tolle, E. (2001). *Practising the Power of Now*. London: Hodder & Stoughton.

Ulsamer, B (2003). *The Art and Practice of Family Constellations: Leading Family Constellations as Developed by Bert Hellinger*. Heidelberg: Carl-Auer-Systeme Verlag.

Ulsamer, B. (2005). *The Healing Power of the Past: A New Approach to Healing Family Wounds. The Systemic Therapy of Bert Hellinger*. Nevada City, CA: Underwood.

Wilber, K. (1998). *The Essential Ken Wilber: An Introductory Reader*. MA: Shambala.

Wilber, K. (2001). *No Boundary: Eastern and Western Approaches to Personal Growth*. Boston, MA: Shambala.

Yalom, I. (1931). *Existential Psychotherapy*. USA: Basic.

Yalom, I. (1989). *Love's Executioner; and Other Tales of Psychotherapy*. London: Bloomsbury.

Yalom, I. (1995). *The Theory and Practise of Group Psychotherapy* (4th edn). New York: Basic.

Yalom, I. (1999). *Momma and the Meaning of Life: Tales of Psychotherapy*. London: Piatkus.

Yalom, I. (2002). *The Gift of Therapy: Reflections on Being a Therapist*. London: Piatkus.

Yutang, L. (1939). *The Importance of Living*. London: Readers Union by arrangement with William Heinemann.

INDEX